Scrivener

Christopher Jarman was born in London UK and now lives in Winchester. He spent eight years in the Royal Navy, Fleet Air Arm. He subsequently published many non-fiction educational books during his time as a teacher and lecturer. He has broadcast many talks on the BBC and published over 150 magazine articles on numerous different subjects. He is a qualified pilot and yacht skipper. This book is his twelth novel.

Other novels by Christopher Jarman

Gladd Tidings

Taking Off

Boomcrack

Flotilla

The Libyan Connection

Staggering On

Cocky's Cold War

Columbia River Kidnap

The Admiral's Last chase

The Swami

Ripples from the Sea

Autobiography

Head in the Clouds

The Fleet Air Arm 1952-1960

Scrivener

Christopher Jarman

Wyke Hill Press

Chapter One

'Oi! Come down from there you young devils!'

The two lads clambering inside the cathedral roof froze at the angry tone of the verger below. Davy, the older one put his finger to his lips and then beckoned his friend Jim to follow him further into the vaulted area above the nave. They were used to exploring the roof and knew very well that the heavy-set and sweating verger would never catch them. Between them they had explored every part of the cathedral from the roof to the crypt. They had found every outdoor facility, the carpenter's shop and the mason's yard. They crouched in the darkness but just able to see the   coloured streaks of light thrown on the pillars from the magnificent stained glass windows.

It was their   favourite holiday activity to spend time amongst the joists of the Winchester cathedral roof. Both boys were 14 years old, pupils of the King's School in Romsey road.

'I know who you are, come down now!'

The raucous voice faded gradually as the two boys moved into the more remote sections among the roof beams.

'If we wait twenty minutes, he'll go away or try to fetch someone. Keep still and then we can get down at the far end.' whispered Davy. Both boys tried not to cough from the clouds of dust that their feet had stirred up.

The two of them were completely uninterested in sport or any physical activity offered by school, but their penchant for exploration in and around the ancient city gave them almost as much exercise as any other pupil.

Jim squatted in a dark corner where the leaded sheets came right down to the vertical wall. It was dusty and dirty. He found part of an interior buttress, with a gap between stones large enough to put his hand in to balance himself. This was a new experience. When he and Davy came up before they had played hide and seek, just the two of them. Now they were both hiding from the verger, even though he was most unlikely to climb the circular staircase all the way up to this height.

Jim tried to keep still but he kept falling forwards as he squatted by the stone buttress. He pushed his hand further in between the stones in order to keep steady. He felt something loose at his finger tips and gradually eased it forwards until he could grab it. A shower of small stone fragments and ancient dust accompanied the package until it fell out onto his knees.

'Hey Davy,' he whispered, 'I've found a book, well I think it's a book. Look at this.'

His friend crept across and took the rectangular bundle from Jim's hands. He blew some of the dust away and used his handkerchief to rub it cleaner. It was bound in dark brown leather with some sort of clasp which was rusted, keeping it shut.

'This might be valuable. I bet it's stayed hidden here for hundreds of years.' said Davy.

'Should we take it home?' asked Jim.

'Yeah, I'm going to show it to my dad.'

'But I found it,' protested Jim.

'Well I mean let's both show it to my dad.'

'OK' said Jim, 'my dad wouldn't be interested anyway. Your dad's a lecturer at the university isn't he?'

'Yes, he teaches maths, but he likes old things.'

After half an hour of waiting the two adventurers crept out of their hiding place and down the rear stairways which were generally unused. The steps were their usual entrance and exit to the huge roof space. They found their bicycles and rode to Davy's house on the Romsey road.

Davy's father Phillip Lawson was at home and was intrigued by the book which the two boys excitedly showed him.

'It will have to go back to the Cathedral library eventually,' he said, 'but in the meantime I think I know just the person who would like to see this.'

It was too difficult to open the book as the metal clasp was fixed by rust or verdigris. Phillip was unwilling to try, and considered that there would be someone at the university who had some professional skill to do the job.

The following morning Phillip took the book into college and found his friend Professor Edward Clarke in the history department.

'Can we go into your study for a moment? I have something to show you,' said Phillip.

They sat down at either side of Edward's desk and the maths tutor produced the leather bound book from a plastic Sainsbury's bag and laid it on the desk. It was quite heavy, bound in surprisingly well-preserved leather and was about two inches thick, suggesting that there would be a considerable number of pages when opened.

Edward Clarke was intrigued and when told how and where it had come from, had no hesitation in taking out a pocket knife and springing the clasp in one go. He gently opened the cover and they both saw that it consisted of about a hundred fine vellum pages of closely written text.

'Can you read it?' asked Phillip. The handwriting looked completely illegible to him.

'Yes fairly easily as it happens,' answered Edward. 'I've been doing a lot of research into medieval manuscripts recently. One soon gets into the way of it. Would you mind if I borrowed this and had a good look at it later?'

'Not at all. It's of more interest to you than to me. Just tell me later what it's all about. I suppose it'll have to go back to the cathedral eventually. In the meantime I suppose it's in safe hands.'

Chapter Two

Later that same evening Professor Clarke sat in his favourite armchair at home with a glass of Glenmorangie. He had started drinking single malt whisky when he was first appointed as professor. He considered it the proper thing to do and then he found he actually liked it. He was surrounded by the comfortable evidence of a succesful professional life. The green wallpaper was William Morris' Willowbough. The curtains of the sitting room were the same design. His wife, who had chosen both, was out at choir practice and he was able to relax and open the book.

He looked at the first page which simply read,

Ned Scrivener

His Boke

AD 1395

Then overleaf it began from the top of the page directly,

Edward saw the 14 th century writing at first and then he
began to read it as if it were in a modern printed volume.

§

I was nott above six years olde when I fyrst saw a
woman's secrett parts. Yt was one of the tymes when the
FitzStephen's men arryved in our village...

I heard shouts and the muffled sounds of horses in the
snow and of doors being broken down. From tyme to
tyme the lord of the manor sent his men to check
whether the villagers were stealing corn or wheat; or in
some cases, deer from the forest. The adults were very
frightened. I could understand that, even though I was
only a child and small for my age. Quite often soldiers
stormed into the village and destroyed property and
attacked some women. My father seemed to freeze and I
can see him now standing on tiptoe by the inner wall
looking for all the world like a dead tree. I was terrified. I
remember someone shouting that they were putting
children to the sword. We found out later that it was only
a threat, and that they would never have done such a
thing in truth. Our neighbour Alice was in the   bothan
with my father and me. She had been a good friend to us
for many years, ever since my mother died. As soon as
Eric, the blacksmith shouted the warning through the
open door into the forge, she called,

'Come quickly Ned.' Then she lifted her skirts and
pulled me underneath to hide there. My face was pressed
firmly against a warm nest of soft hair that smelled a bit
like the horses in the yard. It was strange and exciting. I
knew also that it was forbidden in some way, but it felt
safe, very safe.

After a while, the men went away and I was let out. The
room and the village were as quiet as death for an hour
or more. I remember blinking in the cold daylight and
feeling disappointed and vulnerable for quite some time.
It was a few years before I found myself in such an
enviable position again. By then I did not need pulling in,
but was old enough to instigate the activity myself; and
not with a woman five times my age either. But I leap
ahead of the story here. It is just that this particular
memory always…but no matter.

I cannot recall the next few years so clearly. My father
worked as an assistant to the blacksmith. It was his
function to keep the fire burning, to fetch fuel and to
work the bellows. He was never paid in money, but mostly
in hard blows and the Lord's name taken in vain. We ate
at the blacksmith's table and I was fed only on the scraps
that were left. We lived rent-free, however, in a one-room
bothan at the back of the yard. By the time I was nine or
ten, I was able to help by taking even the largest horses
from their owners quite easily and to look after them and
bring them to be shod. I knew every horse for miles
around. I never felt any fear of the beasts nor they of me.
The person I was afraid of was the blacksmith, Eric. He
was a huge strong brute of a man with a short temper.
My father was meek and obedient and had learned Eric's
ways. He served his master well. Being young and
unforgiving in those days I was sometimes ashamed of
the way my father allowed himself to be ill used. When I
wanted to protest at an unfair criticism or a sudden blow
across the back that he had been given, I was ordered to
shut my gob and to follow his example. I am sure it was
from him that I learnt to keep my own counsel and to
make an outward show of conforming, even when being

treated unjustly. I could see even then, how an advantage could be gained by concealing one's true feelings, while working quietly to achieve a greater end.

Winters and summers followed one another but made little difference to our lives, although the winters could be most terrible because we never had enough food to keep us warm. As serfs we had little value and unless we were employed at full stretch, no one cared whether we lived or died.

One day a very grand person came to the forge while the three of us were working. Eric was hammering a huge piece of red-hot iron that was part of a broken plough. I ran to take the richly dressed man's mount and greeted him in the French tongue as I had heard other superior people do. I did not know what the salutation meant in those days, but I had mimicked what was said from memory and it seemed the right context in which to use the phrase. He was startled to hear this from a yard boy and asked my name.

'I am called Ned.' I said, and fell on one knee as I had observed the pageboys who occasionally accompanied their masters through the village. The man laughed, but I could sense that it was a sympathetic laugh and not a cruel taunt. He allowed me to hold his fine horse while he summoned Eric to give him some instructions.

'Send the boy up to the manor,' I heard him say, 'I may have a position for him.' And that was the beginning of my new life in the year of Our Lord 1375. The life that has led me to this place today. I never saw Eric or my father, or Alice, his mistress as I now realise, for several years after that.

The day following, Eric reluctantly allowed me to leave. He had no choice. What anyone on horseback said was law. I bade a simple farewell to my father and Alice shed a few tears as she hugged me to her bosom. I had no effects nor baggage and certainly no change of clothes and so the five-mile walk was an easy morning for me. I did not hurry, as it was the first holiday I had ever enjoyed in my life. I saw flowers and different trees that I had never noticed before. There were many more birds and small animals in the countryside than we had in the outskirts south of Twyford. I spent four hours on that journey, exploring the fields and woodland on the way, and no one ever knew.

The finely dressed man, I discovered when I eventually arrived at the kitchen door of the manor, was Justin, the bailiff for the entire FitzStephen manor. The position that he made for me was that of kitchen boy, the lowest member of the household. In my eyes, however, it was like heaven. I slept in the warm kitchen and I had plenty to eat. I even tasted meat for the first time in my life.

Not only was my living more comfortable but I began to see many objects and activities that I had never noticed before. Meals were taken on platters such as clean slabs of wood. The quality at the manor, I was told ate off something called pottery and they had forks. I found that very funny. I also saw many dogs, some were big for hunting, others were for the women to pet.

When I was not required to help in the kitchen, I was told to make myself useful outside. It was not long before I made my way to the stables where I immediately formed friendships with all the horses, most of whom were already known to me. Giles, the Marshall, was pleased to see how well I could handle his precious charges, and within a moon he had asked for me to be part of his staff as well as my other duties. This suited me well, as when I had finished helping with the cleaning I was allowed to exercise several of the thoroughbred FitzStephen mounts. Thus, I learned to ride at an age when peasant boys hardly ever touched a horse, let alone mounted one.

One day I was about to sleep when Emily, Giles' daughter shook me and told me to get up quickly and come to the stables. When I arrived one of the mares was trembling and making a kind of rough throaty sound. It was a difficult foaling. We were all expecting the birth but not just yet. I was able to put my small arm into the mother and gradually helped to turn the foal around. I seemed to know naturally what to do. Eventually it was born and Giles gave me such a slap on the back that I fell over in the hay. I had never felt so happy and a part of a family as on that night.

The Marshal was the first adult I had known who was ever truly kind to me. I often heard him speak to his animals softly in the French language, which was used by the family and by many of the wealthy people around Winchester. He taught me most of the words and orders that he used and I found that I picked up the strange tongue very quickly. I was soon able to converse with him, at least on the subject of stable work and the care of horses. His daughter Emily was a couple of years younger than I was, and Giles allowed us to play together in the few hours that I was not required to work. I had no brothers or sisters and had hardly ever mixed with any other children at the forge. It was either work or sleep in those days. Now, although I was doing two lowly tasks, I was employed by people who understood that life was not all labour and that everyone, even Ned the kitchen and stable hand, deserved some free time. In truth, the family and we retainers, observed more than 80 holy days during the year, which I had never known existed before, and they were in addition to Sundays. In the kitchen, we naturally had less time at liberty than anyone else. People always have to eat, and although some holy days were fasts others were feasts.

I suppose now that I was to Giles the son he never had. One day he gave me a small bow and a sheaf of arrows that he had made himself. It was not a toy and when I was taught how to use it I found I could shoot straight. After a season of practice I shot a rabbit one afternoon. From then on I became quite proficient, and killed a badger and several rats as well as rabbits and hares for the table.

Sometimes we saw the Lord and Lady FitzStephen riding out to church on these holy days. There was a richly dressed girl and a boy of about my own age who rode with them. I heard them referred to as the young Lord Rollo and his sister the Lady Antoinette, but we were not encouraged to show ourselves or to look too closely at our betters. If caught in the yard or the roadside when any of the FitzStephens appeared, we were supposed to doff caps and stand or kneel looking at the ground. I was pleased to do this for I was exceedingly grateful for my new position in the household, and proud to be considered part of the family now.

I was most gratified to have a companion of my own age in Emily. I had never had such a playmate and friend before, and I had known so few children that I had not learned to tease and torment girls as I believe other boys did. It was so wonderful to have someone to share thoughts and to notice the strange foibles and behaviour of many of the adults in the household. It was Emily who showed me how Marta the cook used to drink as much wine as she put in to the sauces. She also noticed that Lord FitzStephen always   favoured certain of the dogs and that they were the ones that grew fattest. Emily noticed how my patron Justin always combed his hair forward across the bald patch he had there. I had never thought to observe people or animals in the close way that Emily did, but she gradually taught me to mark every small detail. We would share our knowledge in the evenings before bedtime, when we could sit in the hayloft over the stable and chatter for a couple of hours before darkness. I think Giles was pleased to have a companion for his daughter, because he often patted me on the head when I was with Emily and he treated me with more consideration than I ever had from my own father, God rest his soul.

As I recall, I was chewing on a knuckle of mutton one evening, sitting on a stool before the kitchen fire; it was in my eleventh year. All my duties were done and I believed that I was free and unobserved until morning.

'I see you are very much at home,' said a voice behind me. At least it was some such comment, I cannot remember exactly for I was startled and alarmed and turned round in a panic. Apart from Giles and Marta, no other member of the house had ever spoken to me. I then saw that it was my patron, Justin, the bailiff. I stood up trembling and bowed my head.

'I have been made to feel at home here sire. I hope my work is acceptable.'

'Your work is very good Ned, you do the labour of two

boys. The Marshall tells me you are also quick-witted.' I said nothing to this as I wondered if I had perhaps said something too sharp and caused offence.

'You are to come with me, I have new work for you tomorrow, but first you are to be washed and dressed.'

I followed the bailiff in no little fear of what might happen to me. He led me through into the main hall of the manor whence I had never entered before. We then went upstairs to a small room where a well-dressed servant, whom I took for a chambermaid, made me take off all my clothes. I was then told to stand in a large earthenware bowl and washed down with a woolen cloth like the horses sometimes were, but which I had never experienced myself. My hair was cut short like a pageboy's and then I was helped to dress in fine linen garments, a green tunic and hose that felt like butter on my skin. There was also a new leather belt and shoes. Justin showed me up a steep staircase to a long low space under the roof where there were four or five empty beds. He made me also carry up my old clothes with me.

'You will sleep here now,' he said.

I asked, 'Who else sleeps on these beds sir?'

'You are the first for many years, since the Black Death took them all away.' As he said this I remember him staring out of the small dormer window that was let into the roof. I realise now that his mind was on the way the world was before the great pestilence. I had to be content with his answer, although I did not understand it at that time.

'What will my tasks be in the morning sir?' I made bold to ask because I supposed it would be something important to the bailiff, as he had seen to it that I was clean and well dressed. He did not answer my direct question but said curtly,

'You must go down to the kitchen in your new clothes to break fast at six o'clock. Then you will come to the hall at seven and wait for me.' He left me alone after that to decide in which cot to lie and to try to sleep. I know that we all come from dust and that to dust we shall return, but that night, sleeping in a real bed for the first time in my life, and with fine clothes beside me, I felt like a prince.

Chapter Three

Professor Clarke was completely captivated by the story. In all his experience as a history teacher, he had never read anything so direct as this man's autobiographical journal. At eleven thirty his wife entered the front door. He heard her shaking the rain from her umbrella before she came into the room.

'Had a quiet evening darling?'

'Quiet? Just wait till you read this! It's extraordinary!'

Edward Clarke jumped out of his chair to point out some of the passages in the book. Diana Clarke's specialty was music, not history nor calligraphy and so after a brief look and a smile of approval, she went into the kitchen to make coffee for both of them.

The professor read on...

§

I awoke at cockcrow and rose immediately trying on my finery and strutting magnificently around the empty roof space. I was looking forward to showing them to Emily and to the Marshall. I had no means of knowing when it was six o'clock and so I went down to the kitchen before full daylight. Marta was stoking the fire and boiling water.

'Oh young sir! You startled me,' she said, as I entered from the inside door. Then she realised who it was and exclaimed. 'Mother Mary! It's you Ned!' Then I told her quickly what had happened. She was astonished and had to sit and have a swig of wine from the cooking jug that always stood in a cool corner.

'You do look the part though,' she admitted, and she made sure I had a good meal of oats and a jug of milk.

The sundial in the stable yard shadowed at seven when I walked into the hall and stood at the side waiting for the Bailiff. It was at least half an hour before anyone else came, and then it was a severe looking monk, in a black habit, whom I had never seen around the manor before. He beckoned to me without saying a word and I followed him through a door and along a passage lined with wood panels. We entered a light and pleasant room containing a lectern and two benches at a long table.

'Sit there,' I was told and pushed onto one of the benches. After about twenty minutes the bailiff entered from another door, and with him was the boy I had sometimes seen riding to church, young Lord Rollo.

'Good morning Brother Patrick I trust you are well?' said the bailiff smiling. He turned to the boy and introduced the monk, saying, 'This is your new tutor my lord and here is your companion for lessons, Ned.' He indicated my presence with a brief hand wave.

'Whipping boy you mean,' said Rollo looking at me and grinning maliciously. He sat on the other bench and put his feet up on the table. Justin immediately responded in a severe voice.

'Lord Rollo, your father has said you are to work hard at your learning. Any reluctance or laziness on your part will be brought down upon your *own* head and not upon this boy. If, when Lord FitzStephen himself examines you and you are found wanting, it will be your backside and not this boy's that will smart.'

At this reprimand the young lord sat up straight and looked so apologetic and crestfallen that I could not suppress a nervous laugh. I had never heard someone of quality being spoken to in such a fashion before. I was, however, becoming worried because I had already heard of these so-called whipping boys. It was said that they could be beaten for a rich pupil's errors because it was unlawful for a tutor to touch the members of such families. I looked towards Brother Patrick for some sort of re-assurance, but found in his expressionless face no comfort at all. Justin then left the room and the first lesson I ever received in my life began with an introduction to Latin.

Brother Patrick was a good tutor and I found it just as easy to pick up this new subject as I had the French spoken by Giles. It was soon obvious that Rollo was not only a slow learner, but both arrogant and lazy too. It was true that Brother Patrick was not allowed to flog the young lord and from time to time I was given the end of a leather belt in his place, but the tutor was pleased with the way I responded and never hurt me too much. He explained to me privately one day, that every young lord or knight was expected to have a whipping boy, but that the much smaller population in Hampshire since the plague, meant that such boys were hard to find among tradesmen and merchant's families, so that these days it was not unusual to use a peasant boy such as myself.

'You must be grateful,' he said, 'you will receive the same learning as your young master if you pay attention.'

I revelled in becoming a scholar. We were taught both to read and to write in English, Latin, Greek and French. This also meant learning how to cut a goose wing-feather penna and for this I was presented with a heavy bone handled pen knife that I have kept to this day. We were taught how to make ink from oak galls and iron nails in rainwater, and how to make it glossy if required, by stirring in our own earwax. Rollo usually disdained to carry out these practical tasks and I had to make ink and cut pens for both of us. This also applied to some of the translation work that he was too lazy to attempt. In the end it meant that I gained double the practice in all these things and became more than usually proficient.

Rollo never played with me or ever spoke other than to order me to do something. I did not find this strange, as he was far too high above me in rank for me to expect anything else. However, I gradually became aware that even though I was a poor boy and of no account, I was considerably superior in wit compared to Rollo. It took me a year or two to realise this, but Justin and Brother Patrick had evidently seen my potential early on. It was clearly not to my own or to my family's credit, but a gift from God, which, like the parable of the talents, ought not to be wasted.

One day we had both been working our hardest to perfect our copies of a letter supposed to be written to our parents. Brother Patrick had been teaching us the *Litera curialis,* which was in those days the handwriting style favoured by the courts of justice and by businessmen. He left us alone in the schoolroom for a while. Rollo had paid little attention to the state of his pen and his letter was an untidy scrawl. I had almost perfected the hand with a crisply cut goose quill and was about to lay it upon the tutor's desk when Rollo leaned across and deliberately flicked a penload of ink across my page making it totally unacceptable. I confess that I lost my temper, which had been sorely tried for many weeks, and I punched him in the face just as Brother Patrick returned. Rollo howled in pain and ran out of the room screaming that he would tell his father. Patrick of course, realised what had happened immediately and told me that he would not punish me for the inkblot; we would put it down to Titivillus, the patron devil of scribes.

In a few minutes Lord FitzStephen, to my great fear and surprise arrived with Rollo beside him. His face was red with anger. He ignored me and approached Patrick directly.

'What have you allowed to happen while you were supposed to be in charge here?' he thundered.

'My Lord, it is just a bit of rough and tumble between boys, quite normal I assure you.'

'Show me the work they were doing.'

Lord FitzStephen took the two letters and studied them

for a minute or more. Our names were at the bottom of each paper, clearly identified.

'This is no rough and tumble. You have allowed this snivelling idiot of a son of mine to become so far behind in his studies that he has to spoil another boy's work. It is no wonder he got a blow to the head. I shall give him another myself.' He turned to me unsmiling but in a softer tone.

'You should not make a habit of striking your betters my lad, but this time I agree that you had cause.' I bowed low and stayed as still as I could. When I raised my head, I saw in the background that Rollo was looking at me with the eyes of a devil. He had wet his hose in fear and from that day on I knew I had made an enemy.

During the next four years, I remained friends with Giles and with Emily as I still had my duties to perform in the stables, but I was no longer a kitchen boy. Nevertheless, Marta would always welcome me into her domain and find me small treats and tidbits to eat. My education proceeded apace and I drew so far ahead of Lord Rollo that, although I regret having to say so myself, it became difficult to remain carrying out schoolwork of the same standard. Brother Patrick gave me many extra tasks, which I enjoyed more and more with each challenge.

One afternoon I was out on the Winchester road on a bright sunny morning with only a light breeze, exercising Starlight, one of the horses for Giles. Suddenly a small but beautifully decorated cart drawn by a fine grey came up behind me unannounced and frightened my steed so that he reared up and I was thrown. As I lay with all the breath punched out of me but with no other effects, the cart stopped and a priest jumped out and ran over to where I was trying to catch my breath.

'Are you alright boy?'

He sounded very concerned.

'Where are you from? I will take you home.'

By this time I guessed that Starlight had galloped the two miles back to the manor, and so I accepted the offer. As we rode home I told the priest that I came from FitzStephen's and as he then addressed me in Latin, I replied courteously in that language. He also confided some brief questions to me in French that I answered as well as I could. On reaching the main entrance gate, I asked to be set down so as not to take the stranger too far out of his way, and we bade one another goodbye.

A week later, Brother Patrick told me that Lord Rollo would no longer be taking his lessons in the schoolroom, and that as a result my education too was ended. My tutor was sad and disappointed and I also wondered what would become of me now that my use as a whipping boy was over. I resigned myself to being a mere stable lad again. This was, after all, considerably better than my circumstances with Eric and my father had been, so I was content to slide back into my former life. I had received four years of education, which I would otherwise never have ventured to hope for, and three good sets of clothing and two pairs of shoes. I determined that in a years time, when I became sixteen, I would leave the manor and seek employment as a clerk in a merchant's house in Southampton or Winchester.

I had only spent a day or two making these plans for myself when Justin the bailiff sent for me to meet him in the great hall. When I arrived, he was accompanied by our master himself Lord FitzStephen, and to my surprise, the priest whom I had met on the Winchester road. I knelt before them all and stayed on one knee waiting for instructions.

'Is this the boy?' I heard Lord FitzStephen ask the priest.

'Indeed so my lord, it is the same boy.'

Lord FitzStephen then roared with laughter and told me to stand up and face them all. At this point I became worried as to what sin I had committed. I supposed that I should never have presumed to ride in a priest's cart, but then I thought in my own defence, I had been invited to do so. To my amazement I then heard my lord speak my name.

'Ned, you must know what has happened. When you rode with the Bishop you impressed him mightily with your wit and learning. He then imagined that you must be my son Rollo.' Lord FitzStephen then laughed loud and long again and even Justin smiled indulgently. He continued,

'Bishop William has started a school in Winchester for poor boys and he thought to seed it with one or two sons of more gentle birth to set an example. He asked for Rollo to attend the school, but when I sent him there a few days back, it was apparent that it was not the boy his Grace had hoped for.'

At this point I was beginning to see which way the wind was blowing and could hardly contain my excitement! Why, this was the kind of opportunity that I had not even envisaged, let alone prayed for. I held my breath in anticipation of the next few moments.

'So fetch what chattels you have, and go with his Grace,' said Justin, 'and do not forget to thank Lord FitzStephen for his generosity in letting you go.'

I stammered my thanks and sank on one knee again. My lord patted me on the head and said,

'We have manufactured you here in this house Ned and so I am proud to let you go. Mind that you do us honour in Winchester.'

As I bowed and turned to leave, I saw Rollo standing by the open door that led to the schoolroom. On his face was such an expression of malevolence that I became terrified and ran back to the stable block where I had been so recently relegated, gathered up my clothing and pen knife and without saying goodbye to either Giles or Emily, ran to the Bishop's cart which was standing in the yard.

Chapter Four

My years in the new school at Winchester were among the happiest of my life. I had never seen a city before, and the day I arrived with Bishop William is imprinted on my mind for ever. Firstly, we came through the huge western entrance that was made in the walls, fashioned of enormous stones and with two great wooden gates, which, as far as I could tell, were always open. It was the smell that hit me. Being from the country I had never smelled sewers and such a mass of humanity before. I was told later that it was also the tannery that spread its acrid fumes across the city. Then, I simply could not believe the size of the cathedral when I saw it. It was truly the largest object outside of a storm cloud that I had clapped eyes upon. It was indeed, built to the glory of God.

I was housed in the Priory next to the cathedral, and when I had been settled in and shown the upper floor where the poor scholars slept, the monk who had taken me in said I was free to wander anywhere I wished until the evening meal. Tuition was over for that day and would not begin again until after prayers at six o'clock the next morning. I soon found my way into the city by following the unfamiliar yet tempting sounds and walked down the sloped High Street looking into the myriad stalls and workshops that lined the way. I had no money, as in all my short life I had never been paid or given even a penny for myself. I could see that without it there was nothing I could obtain from the marketplace or from any of the stalls. I was beckoned and called over by several stallholders and I went eagerly expecting some civilities or perhaps a sample of the cooked food that was on offer. It soon became obvious however, that my good clothing from the manor had made the shopkeepers think that I was either wealthy or well connected. When they realised their mistake I was briskly waved away, or even in one instance, a fat older woman took a broom to me as if it was my fault that she had misunderstood my station.

After wandering about the city I soon became familiar with its ways and I   marvelled at the ingenious methods that had been used to divert the river Itchen into different brooks for different purposes. One stream provided the fullers with their supply to felt cloth, another stream was used by tanners for the large amount of leather being finished. Then a third stream was clearly serving as a laundry with washerwomen all along the banks. By suppertime I was back inside the Priory and settled down to a board with a trencher of cheese, horsebread made from beans and oats, and onions with a pint of good ale, far superior in my view, to anything I had been given at the manor. Thus ended my first day at William of Wykeham's school. There were eleven other poor scholars, but I kept away from them to begin with, as they seemed coarse mannered and ignorant, even by the standards of my young master Rollo.

I recall the next day just as clearly for it was my first taste of what it was like to be at a proper school and to be a pupil in my own right, not just a whipping boy and serf. The tutors that taught us were strict but fair. Brother Robert was in charge. If you could show that you were working at your best they would even give praise from time to time. I determined to become the best scholar in the group. To my great surprise however, the boys whom I had taken to be ignorant and uncouth were clever and resourceful. Although I had the better fist in creating my letters with a pen and ink, some of the others were more advanced in reading, especially in Greek and French. There were new subjects to be learnt now, astronomy and music and the works of the ancient philosophers, none of whom had I ever encountered.

Brother Aleric taught astronomy and on the first day asked me the name of any star. I replied Venus, and it was mortifying when the entire class laughed out loud.

'They laugh Ned, because Venus is a planet,' he said kindly, but I burned inside with shame at not knowing such a simple thing. I had thought when Bishop William invited me to his new school that I would be something of a shining example to the others, and here on my first day I had been demeaned. The teaching about Venus stayed in the front of my mind, but deep down I learned the much more important lesson of humility and how pride goeth before a fall. I resolved there and then never to be caught out again. If I could not feel humble inside at all times, I could nevertheless give the external appearance of being so. Thus I would in future avoid the degradation of being found wanting in knowledge. Also, in Rhetoric and in Logic classes, I found out how to resolve a question with another question, which often saves the necessity of knowing the answer. Few of the other scholars appreciated these subtleties as I soon discovered; much of their energies being taken up with playing pranks upon one another and upon some of the luckless older monks.

I have only a few such isolated memories of my years at William of Wykeham's school, for on the whole they were happy and fruitful. I was eager to learn and eventually I became the senior pupil and began to assist in the teaching. I had always been interested in the forming of good letters and by the time I was eighteen years of age I had the honour to become one of the team of scribes that worked in the cathedral scriptorium itself.

I was strong for my age, perhaps because of my early rough upbringing, I was now also taller than average. Maybe it was because of this that Brother Robert, who was a renowned amateur bowman, soon persuaded me to join the local assembly of archers who practised every week in response to the King's order to keep the local supply of fighting men in trim, ready for any call to arms which might come. As an apprentice lay scrivener, I was not a priest or churchman, and as liable for duties on the battlefield as any man. But, like Brother Robert, I soon became enthralled with the power of the longbow, and the skills it engendered, purely for its own sake. I had no thought of killing anyone, least of all the King's enemies who were quite unknown to me. The placing of a shaft into the centre of the target however, that was enormously satisfying. After a year or so, apart from Brother Robert, I was as skilled as any of the group…

Chapter Five

I discovered that the cathedral and city life of Winchester suited my nature well. I was nobody, eighteen years of age and had come from nowhere and possessed no important family connections. It was entirely incumbent on myself to make my own mark upon the world. Amongst the varied population I became just another citizen who had arrived hoping to succeed. Life was so different from the village of Twyford where I had once lived. I saw my old mentor Justin, the bailiff about once every month when he came into the city on business for the FitzStephens. We would meet in the God Begot Inn where he would be pleased to buy me a mug of ale. He would usually give me intelligence of Emily, now in her 17th year. She was unmarried and was working within doors for Lady FitzStephen.

One day I borrowed a horse from a cathedral priest and went back to find my father and Alice. It was vastly amusing to see Eric, of whom I had once been so terrified, run out to greet me and to take my mount. He looked much smaller than I had remembered and had no recognition in his eyes. He was astonished when I asked to speak to the serf who worked the bellows, but stood aside politely enough while I spoke to my father, who, of course did not   recognise me either. I enquired after his health and while I was speaking, Alice emerged from the bothan and ran over at once. She saw right away who I was and embraced me with tears in her eyes. I whispered that I now lived in Winchester and could be contacted at the scriptorium. I then rode away before Eric or my father could waylay me. That was the last I ever saw of them.

I then turned the horse towards the big house and sought out Giles the Marshall in the stables who greeted me royally. He said he had received reports of my activities from time to time from Justin. He was very pleased to know that I   practised archery. He reminded me of the small longbow he had fashioned for me and how I had become skilled at hunting small wild life. He also spoke with a knowing look, of his daughter Emily and how he surmised she would be pleased to see me. I should go into the old kitchen and Marta would fetch her.

When Emily came into the kitchen, she was passing shy compared to how we used to be when we played as children. She actually curtsied as if I was quality and not her old friend Ned. I took her by the hand and led her out of the kitchen door into the yard with the chickens and ducks. This made her laugh and soon we were exchanging gossip merrily like old times. It seemed that she also had been taught to read and to write by Brother Patrick. In the short time we had together that day we vowed to write to one another when we could.

§

Professor Clarke laid a strip of newspaper as a marker between pages and put down the leather bound volume reluctantly on a side table. He thought that this diary or journal was among the first pieces of writing in England to read like a novel. It seemed to be contemporary with Chaucer's Canterbury tales which was published, as he recalled, in 1387. But this was much more modern in its language and full of local references and descriptions of manners and attitudes. His immediate thought was to research the author in some way and perhaps publish the book with his own annotations on behalf of the university. However, he would have to find out the legality and propriety of doing so. With these thought buzzing around his head he went to bed.

In the morning he took the book to his study in college to read further and to show it to his friend Dr Amelia Gillies who was a junior lecturer in medieval history in his own department. She was more than a friend for they had been lovers ever since Amelia had been one of his PhD students.

As soon as Amelia had read a couple of pages she exclaimed,

'But this is gold! Where did you get it Ed?'

The professor explained how the two boys had discovered it in the cathedral roof and that it had come to him via Phillip Lawson in the maths department.

'You'll have to publish this. It's contemporary evidence of that period about life in this area. It presents relationships and education and goodness knows what else. I'm dying to read the rest.'

'Yes I know and I was hoping we might do it together, a joint project.'

'Gosh I'd love to. You are sweet to think of me.'

'Why wouldn't I darling? I think about you all the time.'

Edward Clarke locked the study door and the pair consummated their almost daily coupling on the leather sofa which Edward had bought for this very purpose. There were three separate knocks on the door during this time and each caller went away with the generally accurate view of the department concerning the professor and Amelia's activities in the mornings.

§

I rode back into Winchester well pleased with my visitations.

Brother Robert was waiting to greet me. He gave me the news that the uprising of serfs in Kent and in London a few weeks ago, had not been entirely settled and that the bishop had promised to send some support from Hampshire to the boy King Richard. Brother Robert, myself and six others were to ride to London and join the King's regular men. While I had no notion what the disputation was, I was young and always in search of adventure and pleased to be asked to undertake such a manly duty.

The next day I was given a longbow of my own and a sheaf of two and twenty arrows. I was also provided with a short sword and a dagger for my belt. We were to be paid 3 pence per day plus the loan of a horse each to travel to London. I think that a local landowner was ordered to lend the horses by the kings-man who had travelled to recruit us.

The ride to London took us through Alton and Guildford

which were fine towns but not as imposing to my eyes as
Winchester. It was June and all the lofty trees towered
over us menacingly as we rode. On the other hand wild
flowers abounded as well as plump pigs, goats and horses.
Sometimes the scent of lilies and marigolds and
delphiniums were enough send us into wilds of
imagination. On the way we were joined by other recruits
until when we reached London we were 50 or more in
strength. We were guided to Blachehedfeld to stand by
the young king. But the serf army led by one Wat Tyler
was too strong for us and we retreated towards the Tower
of London with His Majesty, whom I saw with my own
eyes being not more than 14 years of age. I was ne'er
required to use my bow, for which I thank God as I do
not wish to kill or even harm another.
After a sennight the Winchester group were given orders
to return home. Which we did with good grace for
London was an unattractive sewer and with importunate
and pressing women, I can write no more.

On our arrival back at the priory we were greeted as
heroes, for totally false and overdone tales about us had
been told in the market places and the taverns. Being not
averse to this, we mostly smiled and did not deny our
reputations as soldiers of the king. When one of the
scholars asked me how many men I had killed, I
answered truly that I did not know. Fortunately that
seemed to satisfy him.

Not long after this Brother Valerian the Lymner invited
me to work with him and to learn the art of gilding and
illustration. This was what I had wished to do for a long
time and I agreed willingly. I think he believed that my
short time in London had given me some extra

sophistication that could help in my ideas.

Valerian was a small hunched back scribe aged about 50 years with long silver hair and a wizened face. But he had a mischievous look in his eyes which sparkled and were extremely accurate when it came to drawing and painting.

Now came wonderful weeks of learning of pigments and how to grind them and mix with various oils. I also learned to use gold leaf to illuminate parts of the drawings. There were teams of craftsmen and women, each specialising in laying in colour - limming, preparing gold, drawing by the turnours and writing by scriveners. Until now, I had been specialising in writing alone, and was considered to be proficient. The women turnours were especially nimble in drawing fastidious detail.

The scriptorium was upstairs in the priory building with very large plain glass casements which let in a splendid amount of light. The books of hours and prayer books were being made for rich merchants and their wives and daughters from miles around. The moneys helped to give us a fair living and to pay for the upkeep of the cathedral. Parchment from sheepskin and the heavier vellum from cows were set into wooden racks to keep dry. Many cattle and sheep were bred entirely for the purpose of book making. I was told that the book of Kells made nearly 500 years ago, used the skins of more than three thousand cows.

Valerian showed me all he could do and the secrets of his trade, such as pricking out with a needle through several pages in order to rule guiding lines. After a short while the small holes healed up in the vellum and became invisible.

It was about this time that I heard from Justin the bailiff

that his master the old Lord FitzStephen had died of a pox and that young Rollo had become the new Lord FitzStephen. I found this news dispiriting as I knew that Rollo was nothing like his father, who was firm but always fair. I worried that I still belonged to the FitzStephen family although I worked in the scriptorium. I was sometimes referred to as Ned FitzStephen by the older monks. I determined to try and change my name so that I would not be called back into the service of Rollo in some way.

I spoke frankly to Brother Robert who was the senior person in my workplace and asked if this could be done. He said yes, but he believed I would need to have been living and working away from the family for seven years before I could legally change my name. I had arrived in my present position in the year of Our Lord 1380. It was now 1385 meaning that I had to wait for two more years before applying to the bishop to alter my name. I decided never to return to Twyford until I had done this, not even to see Emily. In the meanwhile I asked all who knew me to address me as Ned Scrivener.

Chapter Six

It was near the hour of midnight one Sunday evening in May. I was awake in my cot in the roof space of the scriptorium, where I then slept alone. The younger scribes were in the dormitory across the close. I could hear a commotion in the yard below. There were hoofbeats and the voice of a woman shouting my name,

'Ned, Ned, for God's sake find me Ned. Ned where be you?' and the like.

I pulled on a cloak and ran down to see what was happening. There was a girl on Providence, a horse that I recognised from the Marshall's stable and two men of the watch trying to catch the bridle but being foiled by the skill of the rider. I ran outside and realised forthwith that it was Emily. I shouted to the watch,

'It is a friend, let her go, she will not vex you. Please let me deal with this.'

I ran up to the horse who stood still straightaway and I handed Emily down. She wore a heavy riding cloak over a thin white dress, her feet in what I thought to be her father's boots. I took the horse who knew me well, and tied his halter to the low fence. I told the watch to leave us and I would see to the lady.

She followed me back to my corner above the scriptorium and collapsed onto a three legged stool that I had beside my cot.

'Oh Ned, I have run away. My lord Rollo tried to...' she burst into a flood of tears and bent her head into her hands.

'Emily my dear, you are safe now. I am so content that you came to me.'

I stuttered more of some such comforting nonsense, I hardly remember exactly. I brought her a beaker of fresh water and made sure she lay down on my bedding. I then wrapped in my cloak lay outside the door on the floor. It was a hard surface but I was too pleased to have Emily in my care to worry about such matters and fell into a deep sleep.

In the morning I asked Brother Robert if we could take Emily on as an apprentice scrivener whereas she could then eat and sleep with the other women. He asked if she could write and I was able to assure him that Brother Patrick, who had been my own tutor, had taught her letters already. So he agreed and after a short test, Emily was indentured that very day.

Later, Justin, the bailiff arrived to find Emily and was made confident by Brother Robert and myself that she was safe. He knew well what had caused her to run and told us that Lord Rollo was content to forget the whole thing as long as the horse Providence was returned. Justin led it back in the afternoon and Emily's father Giles was told of her new status and protection amongst the scribes.

§

Three weeks agon, I did some service to a friend of mine in the scriptorium, Athelstan a bookbinder. He was just betrothed this three months to Kate and expecting a child soon. Eldred, another scrivener and who is a ruffian, paid court to Kate knowing full well that she was bound to Athelstan, who is a shy and rather small man. Eldred pushed the lady up against the wall outside the priory one evening, kissed her and pushed his hand up her skirt. I was passing and saw what was occurring. I pulled Eldred from the girl who was very distressed and struck him in the face and threw him to the ground. I am strong and with right on my side I did not spare the villain. After one or two more hefty blows, Eldred ran away and I helped Kate to the small room where she and Athelstan were living.

And yesterday my grateful friend the bookbinder presented me with a leathern bound book of 100 unused parchment pages. I have never seen such a book before. He tells me that he made it from waste pieces of leather and parchment that he is able to obtain readily.

I have began to write the story of my life in it as I am able to recall. I shall keep it secret because Athelstan has also fashioned a lock, so that I may write frankly. And one day someone, perhaps Emily, will be able to read it and form an opinion of my character. My hope in Christ is that I may be honest.

***

It has been a few months since I last wrote in this book and much has happened in the city and indeed in England. The winter has been fierce and snow has lain thick upon the roofs and the ground for over a month.

Two of our scribes died of the fever and many have fingers so frost bit that they cannot write.

Lord Rollo FitzStephen came to the cathedral close yesterday and was shown round the scriptorium by Brother Robert. Robert well knows my sensitivity about Rollo and so he was at some pains to attempt that his lordship did not come to my exact place of work, but he failed. Lord Rollo walked to the far end of the workplace and looked carefully at each scribe and what he or she was doing. He passed Emily quickly without comment. When he arrived at my lectern he stared at the work and expressed interest. He looked straight at me and I trembled and nearly swooned. He gazed right into my eyes and as sure as Christ died on the cross, he did not recognise me. I appeared as unknown to him as any other lowly person in the city. Of course, had I not already known him, he would have seemed a stranger to me also. It is, after all, some eight years since I was his whipping boy and we had each grown to manhood meanwhile. Needless to say, I was much relieved at the outcome of the visit. I felt as if a vast storm cloud had been lifted from me and the prospect of the two years I had to wait to change my name seemed much less gruelling.

Chapter Seven

'Some parts of this are quite sexy.'
Amelia was reading Ned's journal in her own study in the
history department. Her friend and confidant Trish
Baker with whom she shared the room looked intrigued.
'Is that the old book from the cathedral that you
practically wet yourself over?'
'Yes, Edward and I are going to write an intro and
publish it.'
'Who has the copyright?'
'Well that's the interesting thing. Ed phoned up the
cathedral office yesterday and spoke to the archivist
Tristan Smallwood, apparently he deals with copyright
law for the Dean and Chapter.'
'So what did he say?'
'He said that copyright would belong to the writer's
ancestors normally, and they can hardly be chased up by
now. He was probably a monk and had none, but

anyway, since he has been dead for over 50 years and the manuscript is over 100 years old, the Dean and Chapter will be able to sanction its publication QED!'

'Well bully for both of you. What about the boys that discovered it, do they get a mention?'

'If course, they will be listed at the beginning when we tell the story, we can see that they get some of the royalties. Now get out of my face, I'm reading.'

'And will you and Edward share the rest of the royalties?'

'Certainly not, they will be shared between the Cathedral and the University. We get the academic kudos. I could end up with a principal lectureship.'

'And then will Eddy darling leave his wife?'

'Oh God I hope not. I like the shagging but I don't fancy washing his underwear and cooking his supper. that's wives' work.'

'I always said that you were all heart sweetie.'
Both women laughed aloud. Trish resumed reading her students' essays and Amelia turned over to the next page of the journal.

§

Two years have passed since my last entry and my name is now formally Ned Scrivener. I never before had a last name of my own and it feels good. I but merely had to swear before the bishop's clerk and sign in the parish register, a task of no moment at all.
I am now a skilled guildsman in drawing, limming and scribing and can obtain work in any scriptorium in Europe. I am minded to travel to Italy where the finest and newest work is being done. This is not a rumour, I have seen both books and manuscripts from there and

have been amazed at their quality. Brother Robert, who
has been my friend and instructor for many years, has
said that he will pen me an introduction to a colleague in
Firenze, where they are revising the writing style dating
back from the age of Charlemagne called the
Carolingian or the littera antiqua. This pleases me as it is
so much more easily read than our present Gothick
manner.

Meantime, I must add intelligence of my personal life as
Emily and I have been married for more than a year and
we have a child of six months, a boy, whom we have
christened Justin after my first mentor, who took me from
Eric's forge all those years hence. If I go to Firenze I shall
travel alone, but my friends Athelstan and Robert among
others, will look after my Emily and Justin. Bishop
William has given me his personal blessing and a sum of
20 marks for the family. At which kindness I admit I
broke down and became tearful. He has said that he
wants me to return and to teach all that I shall learn in
Italy to the teams in our own scriptorium.

After many tearful farewells between myself, Emily and
little Justin, On the first of May 1385 I set off to walk to
Dover. My pen knife, ink bottle, this journal and a few
basic pigments were in my pouch. Brother Robert had
arranged for me to keep the sword that I had been given
once before, and Athelstan, my bookbinder friend,
fashioned a leather sheath and belt to carry it. I had but
travelled no more than five miles when I was joined by
two soldiers whom I had met before on my trip to
London. Their names were Ralf and Simon. They were
proposing to travel to France for adventure and maybe to
seek their fortunes. At this time there were many rich
merchants and knights who would willingly employ

English soldiers as body guards or as part of their private armies. Since the Black Death twenty-five years ago, wild bands of villains roamed Europe still causing havoc and mayhem. They were a constant source of fear among godly men and women.

Ralf and Simon were pleased to include me as I was taller than either and with a sword of my own and the ability to read and write. I too was equally content to have two such soldiers accompanying me as I had been somewhat fearful of the dangers of such a long journey. We covered the ground at some twenty miles per day. We found cottages who would shelter us each night, or otherwise we slept in hedgerows. It was the start of May and we were all three young and strong. The weather was fine and it was a joy to see the countryside of England laid out before us with the songbirds in the day and the owls screeching at night. I have never been as free in my life and began to realise that I should have started on this journey years agon. Within a week we had reached Dover and found that there were at least six ships in the harbour that were bound for Calais. By presenting ourselves as potential crewmen in turn to each captain, one of the ships accepted our offer straightaway and we embarked, not only free of charge, but to be paid six pence each for the trip. All we had to do was to look fierce and watch that the other passengers obeyed the orders of the crew. All three of us were so seasick during the brief passage however, that had we been asked to perform any serious duty it would have proved impossible.

On arrival in Calais we left the ship and began to walk south. My ability to speak French and Latin helped us greatly in setting off and Ralf and Simon both were grateful. Ralf was about twenty and had worked as a butcher for a while. He was a quick tempered redhead but friendly and with no harm in him. Simon was equally calm and older by three or four years. He had no training in a craft but had been a soldier in Hampshire for several years. He was stocky, dark-haired and seemed to me to be exceeding reliable. He told me that he had to kill more than five people during the revolt of the serfs in Kent and in London.

As we began to pass through the countryside of France, it became evident that it was similar to our own in the south of England except that it was broader and more open with a wide sky. The oaks and yews were of exactly the same type and so the crows and eagles and swans all seemed so similar to our birds in Hampshire that it was a strange but reassuring experience that God has provided the same creatures and plants across the sea.

By sunset on that first day we came across an abandoned cottage in farmland. It looked as if the owners had been the victims of the Black Death 25 years gone. There was nothing to eat or steal. The place had been empty for a generation. But it was fine to sleep in and we made camp in the main room for the night. We shared our quarters with the same rats and beetles that God had also housed.

Three days later we arrived at Arras. It was the first city any of us had seen outside Winchester and a very fine cathedral had just been finished, not as large as Winchester but well proportioned. It was evident that the main trade in the city was wool. I was keen to discover the scriptorium which is attached to the Abbey of St Vaast, but no access was allowed for foreigners owing to the war with England which was ongoing. The three of us were importuned constantly to buy tapestries for which Arras was famed. The war seemed a long way off and did not discourage the French who would trade with anyone.

After a pleasant night with a meal in the house of a friendly wool merchant, we started early the next morning for the town of Saint Quentin. After two days walking through forest and sleeping under trees, we entered a fine plain with many sheep farms.

A day later we came to the bridge across the river Escaut in the centre of Saint Quentin. There a burly French sergeant with two men-at-arms stopped us from crossing the bridge and asked Ralf, who was ahead of us at the time, who we were and what was our business. Ralf flushed with annoyance, laid his hand on his sword, and looked back at me for help as his French was not good enough to answer the man. I stepped forward, and having overheard the questions, I answered as civilly as I could, that we were English travellers on our way to Firenze. We could pay any tax that was due. The sergeant stated that we were spies and would have to accompany him to his barracks. I recalled the way in which Bishop William always treated difficult men, and I leaned forward confidentially with a gold piece obvious in my hand.

'I am a scrivener your honour, and I travel from abbey to abbey for the Bishop of Winchester. His blessing will be upon all who assist me and my apprentices.' I then opened my pouch and showed him the tools of my trade.

'You will be blessed too if you are able to help us sir,' I added, and handed him the gold piece.

'Go on your way scrivener,' he answered and drew aside to let us pass. Ralf and Simon both bowed deeply as they moved on and we continued, having learned a valuable lesson that served us well a few more times.

It has taken us two weeks to reach the sight of the Alps at

a city called Lucern. However, there is a bloody battle
being fought outside the walls at a place called Sempach.
We know not what the quarrel may be, but Ralf and
Simon have both volunteered to serve in the besieging
army of Austrian nobles. They are to be paid well. I am
camped with a kind widow in a cottage to the north of
Lucerne waiting for the fighting to be done so that the
three of us may resume our journey. The widow, Maria
who speaks some English because she has hosted many
travellers from our country, is a fine cook, as the delicious
smells coming from her kitchen bear witness. She has
agreed to shelter me for a few days in return for writing
some letters for her in French.

During the following day, I heard the unmistakable
sounds of fighting about a mile or two off. I was
exceeding pleased not to be in it. In the evening Simon
came back to the cottage half carrying Ralf who had
sustained a nasty gash in his thigh, from a pike he
claimed. Their side had lost to the army from Lucerne
and of course, they had not been paid.

Maria bound up Ralf's wound and said he should rest for
a week. There was nothing to it but to abandon our
journeying for a while.

Meantime I have been making enquiries for a guide to
take us across the Alps to Italy. Maria said she knew a
family who had been alpine guides for six generations.
She told me where they lived and I walked the two miles
to find them. When I arrived there were merely an aged
father Lejeune, and his 26 year old daughter Perreta. The
only two from the family who had survived from the
black death.

I spoke to old Lejeune in French who told me that he no
longer worked as a guide as the ascent was too much for
him, but that Perreta could do it. She had been over the

pass many times with him.

'The world is changing now and young women are taking many men's jobs,' he said with some pride.
I did not know how to respond. In England such a thing could never happen, even blaming the pestilence which the Lord God had inflicted upon us all for our sins. Surely it would be confounding the sin by employing a woman as a guide?
Perreta had said nothing so far and so I turned to her for her opinion. In French she asked quite calmly,

'How much would you pay to go through the Gothard from Lucern to Ticino 60 miles in all.'
I had no means of knowing this was true, but considered that 60 miles would take us three days. Both Perreta and her father laughed royally at this.

'Three days on the flat plain possibly, but at least a week across the pass in the snow, then I have to walk back maybe without a customer,' said Perreta seriously when she had recovered herself. I thanked the two of them and left to think about the offer.
When I reported the conversation to Simon and Ralf, they both urged me to accept the offer of a woman to guide us.

'We will be legends on our return home,' said Ralf.

'Can she cook?' asked Simon, ever practical.
So we agreed to offer Perreta three pence per day for as long as the travelling took. I returned the following morning to make the bargain. She did not jump for joy but listed the clothing and equipment we would need for the journey. This was strong leathern boots, a tent, long staves for walking among rocks and snow, and food for a week.

'An axe would be of more use than your sword,' she called as I started to return.

'What for?' I asked.
'Cutting firewood you simpleton,' she cried.

The provisions for crossing the Alps took almost half our stock of money; but what else could we do? I had found no other guide willing to take us. It was now the 3 rd of August and by September, many locals said that the Gotthard would be impassable.

On the 4 th of August we bade farewell to Maria and I asked the others to kneel and pray for our souls and the safety of our own loved ones in England. I shed a tear as I thought of Emily and Justin, should I perish on the mountain. What might become of them should our friends, Brother Robert, Athelstan and indeed Bishop William meet with accidents? With such dark thoughts and a great fear of the unknown mountainous road. I set off in a melancholy manner.

Perreta soon cheered us all up. She walked in such a jaunty manner, carrying a pack on her back every bit as heavy as ours and a sturdy long walking stick which looked well used. She had abandoned all fripperies of womanhood and wore men's leather trousers and a leather jerkin. A red coloured woollen bonnet topping her fair hair was her only concession to femininity. It quickly became clear that she was well used to the work and her advice at every turn of the road or unexpected rise was always given with great confidence and experience. She often walked beside me and asked endless questions about England and my work. She asked about my family and even about my health.

The first 20 miles or so were to take us alongside the edge of Lake Lucerne. This was a most pleasing walk with dramatic and sublime views of the mountain ahead of us. We saw snow for the first time this year.

By evening we were at Altdorf, a petite hamlet at the entrance to the pass. There was a pleasant inn where we were all made welcome and given a special price as Perreta was well-known to the landlord. Here we sat and exchanged stories with the local peasants. We were told that their local hero was one Wilhelm Tell who was a native of Altdorf and a wonderful crossbowman. Only 70 or so years earlier, he had refused to bow before the hat of the local Austrian reeve Gessier, which had been placed on a pole in the village for the people to do so. Gessier, to punish him, made him shoot at an apple placed on his young son's head. Which, if he succeeded would save both their lives. Tell split the apple in twain with one shot and was reprieved. I had never heard this tale before and being a keen archer myself, I note it here. It seems to me that the story would make a very nice illustration for a book of hours one day, providing I can discover if Wilhelm was a true Christian.

From hereon the path became steeper and we reached Andermatt said to be over 8,000 feet high. Just before the village we crossed the famous   Teufelsbrücke - Devil's Bridge across the river Reuss which forced us to kneel at the other side and give thanks for the audacious builders who had constructed it 150 years before. We have been fortunate with the weather as so far we have found human shelter for each night with people who know our guide well.

In Andermatt we were given a warm cattle shed with a brick fireplace. After a meal with the farmer and his family, the four of us were escorted to the shed which had hay on the floor making it comfortable. It was not so warm at 8,000 feet, and so while Perreta and myself were left to make up some beds of hay, Ralf and Simon went off into woods with an axe to collect firewood.

As soon as Perreta and I lay down and relaxed, she took off all her outer clothing and moved over to my hay pile.

'Ned dear I want you to give me a child,' she said softly. I was so surprised that I stood up and backed away.

'Why? What do you mean? Are you serious?' I stuttered a few more questions until she answered me.

'There are no young men any more in my village. The pestilence killed them all, at least those that were suitable. I shall never have a husband. We must have more children and you are tall and strong and educated. I ask you in God's name to make me with child.'

I was completely outraged. What Perreta was suggesting was a sin. I could never betray my Emily in such a way. All her entreaties were in vain. I told her that I was sorry for her plight but these things, like the plague itself were in God's hands. She tried to persuade me and a ridiculous argument ensued with Perreta trying to undress and seduce me, which I admit was very pleasant and tempting, but I resisted. This was partly because of pride I think. I would have preferred to have been the instigator and not the protester.

After a few more minutes Simon arrived with an armful of firewood, quickly followed by Ralf carrying the same. I am embarrassed to think what they might have stumbled over had I agreed to Perreta's proposal. I helped them stoke up the fire before we all settled down in the hay. I could not but wonder which of the other two Perreta would now approach as she seemed very determined. I prayed that it might be on another occasion.

Our next walk was the hardest so far. We were making for a hamlet known as Oriolo. It was only 14 miles away but on a tortuous path, often winding way back upon itself in order to climb or descend more easily. We all made good use of our stout sticks to support us and yet there was many a tumble. Fortunately, we moved below the snow line on this day and the sun also shone warmly on our backs. I felt that we were coming close to Italy by now and nearing the end of our journey. But in this I was being hasty. The mountains were almost behind us, and the land sloped only gradually into the wide plains of the north of our destination country. It all threatened some longer walks to come.

Perreta made no reference to our difficult conversation the night before, neither did I. I cannot say in my heart that I was not enticed, but I feel no guilt as Our Lord was also tempted and passed the test.

In Oriolo we found no-one willing to give us shelter. It was a poor place and with no lights showing when we arrived. So we put up the tent which we had carried between us all the way from Lucern and after eating some bread and cheese lay down together fully clothed inside. All four of us were exhausted from the effort of the winding route. I made sure that both Ralf and Simon lay between me and our guide.

In the morning Perreta said that we did not need her anymore and we could easily proceed on our own. It is true that the road from now on is more straight and simple to follow, but we were all loth to say goodbye. Apart from the incident which I did not share with my companions, she had proved a good guide and a friendly travelling companion. It seems that she has found a pedlar with a cartload of provisions and a good horse who will take her back to Lucerne for free. I paid her what we had agreed and I also wrote out a commendation of her services as a guide on vellum, which the three of us signed. At least Ralf and Simon made their marks and I appended their names.

So now we have started uphill from Oriolo on the long road to Milano. We have to climb for only ten miles and then it will be gradually downhill. Milano should be five days journey according to the folk we asked in the village. I managed to write six letters for people in the square for payment and the other two earned money chopping wood and herding sheep for a day.

Chapter Eight

'Is that young woman working with you on the old book from the cathedral roof?'
Diana's question hung in the air like an accusation in court. Professor Clarke inside his head tried to answer like a barrister.

'If you're referring to Dr Gillies, she's still my main researcher, and a good one. Her knowledge of the 14th century is unparalleled.'
Diana was not subtle, she played what the Americans called 'hardball'.

'I'd say that her knowledge of the ceiling of your study was probably also less than paralleled.'
Her husband was unshaken, this was a game that the two of them had been playing for a couple of years.

'Why use innuendo? If you know something come straight out with it.'

'Do you think that bonking your little friend will aid in her assessment of the value of this ancient text?'

'Dr Gillies is proving very helpful and insightful, I'm delighted to acknowledge her as a colleague. We have a unique treasure here in this bloody book and one day you'll be grateful for what its discovery will do for us all.'

'Boooring!'

'This ancient text is proving a window into the thoughts and mores of a medieval scribe, such has never been seen before. You should be impressed not cynical. It's turning my department into time travellers.'

'Look Neddy, I don't care what your department is turning into. You can mark time there as far as I'm concerned. What *would* impress me would be if you slept at home once in a while.'
'Oh Diana! I had no idea you cared.'

Edward Clarke made his dramatic exit through the front door of the house and walked half a mile to the university. The exchange was something that happened roughly about once a fortnight. Without it, he felt that his marriage would not be complete. Diana was a moderately jealous woman who also had her lovers. He did not refer to them and most of the time she did not refer directly to his. These little flare-ups meant only that they were still solid; but Diana at least, was prepared to send certain warning shots across his bow if she thought he was going too far.
Arriving at his own department quite early in the morning for him, it was ten o-clock, he found a line of six first and second-year undergraduates outside his door.

'Professor Clarke sir, may we have a look at the famous medieval scribe's diary?' 'We've all heard about it.' 'Please sir, don't be mean, we'd all give anything to see it.'
Edward was gratified to be so sought after. He did not normally court popularity. So he agreed and unlocked his door. The students pushed in and waited expectantly. The professor then remembered where the book was. He had allowed Amelia to take it home to finish reading it

last night. He had asked her to make some notes.

He took out his mobile and searched for Amelia's name. He gestured for the students to sit anywhere,

'This is embarrassing,' he said, 'I have to make a call.' He sat on the edge of his desk.

'Ah Dr Gillies, are you in college? Would you bring the scrivener book to my office please?'

There was a pause. The students strained to hear what was being said by Amelia, but no luck. She was telling Edward that the cathedral archivist had come round to her flat that morning and demanded to have the book, saying that no-one in the cathedral had given permission for it to be removed from the building. If she did not give it into his care he would call the police.

Edward closed the phone and told the waiting fans that there was a hold-up and he could not let them see the book for the moment.

'Goodbye, goodbye, off you go shoo...' He waved his left hand in an unmistakeable dismiss. With murmurs of disappointment the little party went back to their usual morning activities of sitting in the common room drinking coffee, and shredding the characters of all the staff members.

Edward phoned Amelia back pronto,

'Now what's all this about the police?'

'It's like I just said, the archivist man came round and was very officious. I had to give him the book. He was rather cute actually'

'Have you read it?'

'Not completely no. It's not as if it's freshly typed. I'm not quite up your your standard in reading the humanistic hands of the 14 th century. In any case, this Ned obviously began to change his style when he got to Firenze, that's what he went there to learn after all.'

Tristan Smallwood, the Winchester Cathedral part-time archivist, normally worked in the Hampshire record office, but spent a couple of days a week in the Cathedral offices in the Close. His conversation with Professor Clarke a few days earlier, had made him suspicious. A few phone calls to contacts at the university soon came up with the story that was going around about the discovery of some ancient diary hidden on cathedral property. This really annoyed and intrigued him. In his experience academics were prone to take manuscripts and deal with them without permission or much thought for preservation. All they wanted was to publish something that would enhance their reputation. He considered it to be his duty to recover the book before it went right out of the custody of the proper owners.

Once in his own hands, he took the precious volume home to inspect it and to evaluate its genuine importance. He was stunned by the story. Even as a history graduate himself, he had never read anything like it before. He was well schooled in the English writing styles of the middle ages and could follow the text even more easily than Edward Clarke. He poured out a couple of inches of Aberlour, his favourite single malt, and after three hours he had perused the diary from cover to cover. He then started to read it once more from the page that Ned and his companions entered Italy for the first time.

§

Our descent into Italy was down a very long valley and as Perreta had said, it was quite simple. We passed under avenues of high trees similar to the evergreens of our own New Forest. Every two or three miles we crept

61

silently through very small hamlets which looked as if the inhabitants were sheep farmers in the main.

One morning as we began to leave the shelter of the great trees I saw a fine example of a yew. I had been told many years ago that the best wood for a longbow was the Italian yew and this example contained many good straight staves up to eight feet in length. I pointed the tree out to my two companions and as it was clearly part of the forest and not owned by anyone, I suggested that we cut a stave each to make ourselves bows in the future. This we did and with three straight yew staves measuring six feet each, we threw away our old sticks and kept the valuable ones to walk with.

After five more days we began to see the outskirts of Milano around us. It was as large a city as London but in the bright sunshine more attractive. As we proceeded into the centre, the buildings became enormous, just as I had imagined them from the illustrations I had seen, but bigger and finer than I had assumed. We were assaulted on every side by beggars and pedlars trying to sell us everything from food to leather belts. The smell was generally of spices and of flowers growing everywhere in pots. There were jongleurs and acrobats too for entertainment. We saw men walking on stilts and occasionally knights in armour riding strong horses. We were accosted several times by boys inviting us to stay at their lodging houses. So eventually we followed one of them to a pleasant courtyard or piazza where his mother welcomed us with a smile and some wine. All three of us were strong-looking and although lightly armed, I know that we were considered to be too brawny to mess with, and so it proved. We had become more hardened and confident from the experiences of our long walk. Both Simon and Ralf had picked up a working knowledge of

French. Now we all had to learn an Italian dialect. Latin served me very well as everyone understood some form of that language.

Our landlady had a merry fellow for a husband who poured out large tankards of beer for us. His name was Adamo and the good wife's name was Cinzia. He told us that he had been brought up to be a monk until the age of eighteen. He then ran away with Cinzia and they had four children. I thought that there must have been a much more complicated story to it than that, but he would say no more but kept putting his finger beside his nose and winking. The three of us spent a week in the albergo with the good couple and their attractive children. We ate and drank like lords and were charged very little for both bed and board. Finally, I said that I must move on to Firenze, but Ralf and Simon both decided that this was where they wanted to stay. The local nobleman was recruiting for a small army and they both wanted to sign up.

With a heavy heart I bade farewell to my two companions who had proved such faithful travellers. We had created a special bond between us and so I left for the road to Firenze alone and lacking their protection and companionship. The road was more open and easy than any we had experienced before, and there were more varied and friendly souls going my way.

It is ten days since I left Milano. I am now settling into new quarters in Firenze. August hath turned to Septembre and yet the weather is almost too hot for one who has been used to Hampshire. I had many small adventures during the walk. There were some temptations which tugged at my conscience sorely. I am vowed to keep faithful to Emily, but my foreign appearance and build seems to appeal to certain Italian maids, especially in Bologna. I verily do not know why. But Our Lord maintained that it is no sin to be tempted.

Firenze is a place like no other I have seen so far. It is so busy and the noise of building work is at the back of every other set of noises. At least half the buildings have scaffolding around them and rich merchants seem to be paying for refurbishment as well as new constructions. In every thoroughfare one passes huge carts of stone being hauled by heavy horses. Most people on the streets and stalls are excited about the new face of the city that is appearing.

I have spent some time enquiring into stationers to discover where the best scribes work and which of all the monasteries would want to employ me. The truth is that I am spoiled for choise in Firenze. It seems that at least one third of the population can read and write, which is hard to believe after Winchester and the other towns I have passed through. Many of the monasteries here are run by the rule of St Francis or of St Benedict. Both of these employ scribes to copy out hundreds of manuscripts.

After a good meal at an inn near the river Arno, I found a bed for the night in a nearby small monastery where they welcome travellers. The brothers asked me many questions about my home and my travels. They were pleased to find that I wished to learn all the latest about documents and illumination. We spoke in Latin as I am finding that there are too many dialects of Italian to make it worth learning any particular one. In the religious communities Latin is very acceptable.

Chapter Nine

Professor Clarke was incandescent with fury. He blamed himself for allowing Amelia to take the old volume home. This made him even more enraged now that she had lost possession of it. Who would have thought that the measly archivist Smallwood could have put two and two together so quickly and then to retrieve the book. And what sort of name was Tristan for God's sake? He stopped being irrational after a moment and began to plan his next move. It was obvious that he would have to go over the archivist's head and at a higher level. He went across to see the Vice-Chancellor right-away.

Professor Julian Smart was a suave and experienced academic. No-one becomes a Vice-Chancellor of a university without political knowhow, diplomatic skills and personal contacts. Julian Smart had all these qualities in spades. Edward Clarke himself was well aware of this and mentally kicked himself for not contacting Julian earlier.

Edward entered the Vice-Chancellor's room in the easy manner that he always adopted with his boss. Julian Smart was always asserting that he was *'primus inter pares'* and so most of the heads of departments took him at his word.

'Good morning Julian, I trust you are fit and well?'

'Good morning Edward I'm fine. How's the Cathedral book discovery going?'

'Ah, I'm glad you asked me that.' Edward sat in the comfortable chair that the office afforded to visitors. Julian rose and came round to sit informally opposite him.

'You're surprised that I knew about the book?' asked the V-C.

'Not at all, I know that you always have your finger on the pulse, but did you know that it has been snatched back by the Cathedral?'

'No by golly, I did not. Tell me more.' Edward told the story of how Tristan Smallwood had taken the book from Dr Gillies. He did not explain why Amelia had the volume, although he guessed that with his finger on the pulse, Julian Smart would have a good idea.

'So you want me to get the thing back for you Ed?'

'Back for us Julian. I had hoped that the University would publish it, with our comments of course.' The V-C stroked his chin and said nothing.

'Come on Julian,' said Edward 'you would desire that as much as anyone surely?'

'Very possibly, but you want me to go to the Dean and Chapter about this and I have to think very carefully before I can do that. I believe you may have gone close to breaking the law by accepting the parcel from two small boys.'

'Oh bollocks! There was no intention of keeping it, just a natural academic curiosity.'

'I will of course, endeavour to put that point of view to the Dean, possibly in a different form.' said the Vice-Chancellor smoothly.

The Dean of the Cathedral sent a note to the Vice-Chancellor inviting him to take tea as soon as he could manage. The two men were old acquaintances. In fact as boys they had both been at the same public school.

Julian Smart walked over that afternoon. He had not made this short walk for some months. On the way he noted how everything about the cathedral and the close seemed to trumpet expense. On entering the deanery he was welcomed by Tristan Smallwood who was clearly the other guest.

The Very Reverend the Dean of Winchester Brian Woodward, rose from his armchair to greet both men. Julian was urbane and the Dean was unctuous. Tristan Smallwood acted like a nervous macaw.

The Dean spoke first,

'Do sit down my dear Vice-Chancellor, Indian or China?'

'Indian if you please.'

'Tristan, will you be mother?' asked the Dean suavely as always. He faced Julian and smiled,

'I gather that your Professor Edwards has had his toys taken away?'

Smallwood sniggered and nearly spilt the cup of tea that he was about to hand to the Vice-Chancellor.

'Oh I wouldn't put it like that exactly, we're talking about an important academic find I think?'

'An important religious find I'd say,' said the Dean with a courtly smile. He reached ostentatiously for the sugar bowl, which Smallwood was anxious to hand him.

'Shall we agree that the book is an important discovery made by one of my staff.'

'Originally by two small boys who were trespassing in our roof,' countered the Dean

67

Julian became angry at this point, much against his will and suppressed it instantly.

'I was assuming I was invited here to discuss rationally what we should do. I for one have yet to see the book and I surmise that it is also the case with yourself Dean.'

'Unfortunately that is so, but my archivist here has read the document and tells me that it is historically speaking very momentous indeed. It may also be financially advantageous to the Cathedral. '

'My dear Dean I appreciate that in every sense and I'm here to say that the interest of the university is entirely of its possible academic significance. When you and your advisers have perused and evaluated it, we would like to be the first to examine it as an aid to teaching and of pure scholarship.'

'I do acknowledge your genuine interest Julian and as soon as we have looked into it I'll be delighted to hand it over for proper scholarship purposes. Would you like a scone?'

§

I have been living in Firenze for a sennight now and finding it a most rewarding experience. The poor monks with whom I stayed on my first night knew very little of the work of scribes, but they were full of gossip about the more well-known clerics and artists. I soon learned that the stationer's shop of Vespasiano da Bistice was the place where all the best scriveners and limmers purchased their materials. I found the property and spent a few hours looking through his remarkable stock of ink galls, quills and all manner of vellum and parchment. Vespasiano also commissions books of hours and documents for rich merchants as far away as Rome and Naples. He consented to speak to me on my second visit and became interested in the fact that I was a fully trained scribe and illuminator from England. He told me that the most advanced scribe in Firenze was probably Poggio Bracciolini who was in charge of several teams notably in the monastery St Maria degli Angeli, and the Santa Croche where an artist called Gaddi was painting frescoes. Needless to say I hurried over to the Angeli straight away with my tools and some samples of my work. When I arrived, there was a busy scriptorium with a friar Matthias in charge. He told me quite rudely that Poggio was away in Rome and he had no time to see foreigners.

This experience was not rewarding and so I went back to Senor Vespasiano's store and asked if he knew any other scriptoria where I might find employment. He said that he had a request for a short exemplar to be written out in a hurry for a client in the city. If I did the request, he would then have seen a sample of my work and might recommend me. I thought it was a good gamble at any rate. I prepared vellum, made new oak gall ink and copied overnight.

Est homini uirtuus fuluo preciosior auro:
Ingenium quondam fuerat preciosius auro.
Miramurq magis quos munera mentis adornat:
Quam qui corporeis emicuere bonis.
Si qua uirtute nites ne despice quenquam
Ex alia quadam forfitan ipse nitet

As soon as Vespasiano saw my slightly old fashioned Carolingian style which we use quite frequently in Winchester, he became enthusiastic.

'This is what Master Poggio Bracciolini is trying to get back to, with his scribes. I know he'll be pleased to see your familiarity with the style. I'll give it to the client, but I beg of you, write it out again for Bracciolini.'

He then muttered a lot in fast Italian which I gathered that he blamed himself for not setting me a test weeks agon. The next day I wrote out the sample again on a fresh piece of vellum and added a few drawn swirls of wild flowers in colour.

I was encouraged by the stationer's attitude, and straightly found myself a clean lodging in the piazza outside the St Maria degli Angeli. The landlady was a middle aged woman called Lucia Bonavista whose cooking smelled heavenly. She had a beautiful dark-haired grand daughter called Isabetta who helped with the chores. I was given a large room freshly painted in ochre with a matrimoniale, which is what the Florentines call a double bed. I was provided with a table and chair and a large coffer under the window. The window overlooked a small but well designed courtyard with a well in the centre and many sweet smelling flowers in pots.

I heard that Poggio had returned from Rome and by waiting at the door of the monastery I obtained a short interview with the master. I mentioned the name of Vespasiano and handed him the vellum sample. I was delighted to hear him turn to the scribes in the room and say,

'Here my children, is an Englishman who can write like an angel.' He spoke in French and of course I understood every word.

'This scrivener has quite naturally achieved what I have been asking you all to do for the past six months.' Poggio shook my hand and insisted in walking me around the room and introducing me to his top students. In particular, I recalled the scribe called Matthias, who had been so dismissive of me when I last called. I saw the look on his face that immediately reminded me of Rollo when we were boys.

'This one is going to be jealous of me whatever I do' I thought. I determined to praise him and to win his affection before too long.

Poggio offered me a place on his team at a salary I could never have made at home. Yet the price of food and board here is less than England.

***

It is three moons since I last had any leisure to write in this journal. I have become quite domesticated at my quarters with Signora Lucia. But today I must note what happened early this morning. My old companion Simon arrived at the door with his new wife, having walked here from Milano, what a surprise!

Her name is Lisa, and Simon has taken a new surname for his married status. He is Simon Martial now. He became tired of soldiering for very little pay and had turned to crafting with wood. He has also learned to read and write. While he was in the local army he began carving practice swords, and making arrows for the crossbows. One or two nearby families asked him to make beds and chairs and chests. He has become successful enough to marry and to move to Firenze. He has offered to pay me to write a series of handbills, advertising his skills, which is why he and Lisa came looking for me at once.

My own work is only partially successful, because my suspicions of the senior student Matthias have proved correct and he slanders me and makes trouble as often as he can. I always attempt to act pleasantly before him and not to respond to his taunts, but it is difficult to be restrained. Nowadays, I go home immediately after work and spend some blissful time with Isabetta my landlady's grand daughter who is only 17 years old. She has the looks of a young madonna. She is attentive and a welcome companion after the strains of work. I am teaching her to speak and to read English. As she has never been to school, she now inhales new knowledge like someone who has been starved of air. I do not believe she has forgotten one iota of what I have taught her. She in turn is teaching me the local form of Italian and also how to cook some Italian dishes peculiar to this part of Firenze. In particular something known as pasta which is widely held to be the finest food in the country.

Simon and Lisa have found lodgings nearby and he has a store room and small workshop. My landlady's late husband was a wood worker and shipwright, making boats to sail on the river Arno and she has sold his collection of tools to Simon for his new business.

Simon came over the other night and showed me the excellent longbow he has fashioned out of the ash staff that he cut from the alpine forest.

'Have you still retained your ash stave?' he asked me. I replied,

'Of course, it has been maturing in my room very nicely. One day I intend to make a longbow myself.'

'Oh no, you must let me make it for you. I've learned the hard way how to do it and I need to make another to perfect my apprenticeship.'

And so Simon has begun to make me this very English weapon of war. I watched him yesterday shaving the whole length of the branch sliver by sliver with a sharp drawknife. He has to keep the heartwood for the back of the bow, which is depressed when firing, and the harder wood for the front which is stretched and sprung. I find that the Italians, like the French see their crossbows as superior because they are mechanical. But I suspect that their archers are not strong enough to pull the full bow. In England all men practice every week from a young age and perfect the muscles needed.

Although we are both retired from soldiering, I can see that Simon is as excited as me at the thought of another means of defence in these uncertain times.

I am now copying part of a book under Matthias' leadership. In truth it is is very easy as I have manufactured my own ink from the copious number of oak galls to be found in Firenze. I drop half a dozen galls into a jar of rainwater and a small handful of copperas, which we make by soaking old nails in sulphuric acid. With the sun in abundance in Italy. I can leave this mixture on a window-sill until it becomes a fine *encaustum*, which when used as ink, will just burn itself enough into the parchment to stay   permanent. There is no need to use my own earwax as we did with brother Patrick. I can obtain good quantities of acacia gum in Firenze to help with fluidity and a little gloss.

Every day I meet with some sarcastic comment from Matthias and I am cautious about where I leave my ink horn, remembering what Rollo once did to my work with his anger. Although as a good scribe, I doubt that Matthias would vandalise our work. He will, I am sure, find some other way to discredit me among our colleagues.

My little pupil Isabetta is proceeding very well and we can have simple conversations in English about things that please us, or about the household. She finds the writing more difficult, and I believe that marks one of the many differences between men and women. She does not see the point of writing language down. She says that if she can say it, why write it? I have to agree with her to some extent. I only started to write when I knew I would be paid and I also wanted to read books written by wise men before me. For Isabetta there is really no reason for her to write or to read, unless it be necessary to send messages in secret to one another, and for that I see no possible need.

Simon has begun to bring his longbow and his own 30 inch fledged arrows over to me on a Sunday. We then walk out to a nearby field which is common land and unfenced, very like a Sunday morning in Hampshire. He has fashioned a light target of a stuffed bag of hay resting on a triangle of wooden legs. We each reckon we are accurate archers up to 200 paces and so we both rehearse and compete. To begin with, Simon was much better than me, I was so out of practice. But these past few weeks I have improved and now there is little between us. When he had finished my longbow, he brought it with him and a dozen well wrought arrows and we were able to compete using our own bows. There was no doubt that the latest model, made for me was slightly lighter and also stronger. I proposed lengthening the butts to 250 paces. Simon laughed and repainted the circles on the target. He used yellow for the bull's eye which is only a hand's breadth across and at 250 paces hardly visible. However, we persevered for several months in the fancy that were reliving our youths on an English Sunday afternoon. I have been hitting the bull at least six times out of ten and Simon, who cannot stop laughing for the joy of it all, has a regular score of five.

We have taken young Isabetta out with us two or three times, but she cannot even draw back the bow more than two inches and has an attack of mirth at the same time as Simon, which does not help.

Master Poggio has announced that the pope himself, Boniface IX, proposes to visit us here in Firenze. I was told that there are now three popes, and that this one was the true pope as he was acknowledged in England. I know nothing of these high-up people and their doings, but evidently this important man, just having been newly elected, is to visit our monastery and will be viewing our work. I became very morose once I had considered the news. I have heard that scribes in the past have been executed for activity that annoyed the Church. But Master Matthias in an unexpected burst of amity told me that this pope was illiterate and so hardly likely to pretend to read what we were writing. But, I saw in his own eyes something more akin to relief than goodwill.

When the great day of the visit came, all the monks were in their best white scapulars over newly washed habits. We lay people were asked to wear something clean and to be either showing a full beard or be clean shaven. His holiness was surrounded by armed men and as he passed by me in the scriptorium I smelled wine and body odour combined, which put me straight in mind of the old Lord FitzStephen at Twyford, rest his soul. The moment was soon past with only a cursive look at the many samples that Master Poggio had so carefully laid out.

When the whole troupe had left the building, it transpired that one of the vellum samples had been taken as a souvenir for Boniface IX by the pope's secretary, and indeed it was one of mine. I was astonished to be thus recognised and fell to my knees with gratitude and joy before Master Poggio when he gave out the news. As we left to go home afterwards, I could feel the hateful eyes of Matthias on my back. There was no need for speech. I knew then that I had further enraged my enemy.

Chapter Ten

Coming out of a successful Chapter house meeting on a warm spring day was one of the private delights of Dean Woodward. Suddenly, there were hundreds, if not thousands of bright chrome daffodils splashed across the Winchester cathedral green. After this particular meeting, Brian Woodward almost saw the little flowers as gold sovereigns scattered voluptuously across the grass. The meeting had been entirely about 'the book' or 'Ned's Journal' as he was thinking of it in his mind. The remarks of the man from Sotheby's whom he had invited to address the chapter still rang in the Dean's ears.

The Honorable Sir Quentin FitzStephen, who was the 14th century expert from the prestigious auction house had called the journal 'unique', 'unprecedented', and probably worth two or three million pounds in an international auction. However, in his view, it should be given to the nation... at which point the Dean had stood up thanked Sir Quentin heartily, whispered to the minuting secretary to leave out the unofficial valuation, and asked all present to put their hands together in gratitude to Sir Quentin for his opinion. The book had been passed round for everyone to see for themselves and to marvel that a humble layperson over six centuries ago could have opinions too and to write them down.

Canon Felicity James followed the Dean into the sporadic sunlight and caught up with him. He carried the precious volume wrapped in a silk handkerchief and placed into his best pigskin briefcase. Felicity spoke in those particular vowels that arise along the Thames estuary, and which irritated the Dean in an uncharacteristic way and also shamed him deeply.

'This is so exciting Brian,   heow clever of you to discover the journal and to foind the roight expert to tell us all abou' it.'

'Thank-you Felicity, you are very kind.' The Dean waited a few more steps for what would inevitably follow any initiative of this particular canon.

'I was finking, wouldn't it be a wonderful idea to make the book into like a play, sort of a medieval mystery play. I'd be 'appy to...'

'Thank-you so much, I am sure you would Felicity. Don't you think a better term might be a   *miracle* play rather than a mystery in this case?'

'Heow appropriate Brian. Yes I'll have to fink about that. What a good oidea.'

'Yes please think about it and let me know.' the Dean increased his pace. He turned to call over his shoulder,'

'Love to your better er - other -I mean Gillian.'

Canon Felicity James felt a cross between elation and confusion, as she always did in her brief exchanges with the Dean.

Dr Amelia Gillies was waiting in Professor Clarke's office

when he arrived back the morning after he had visited the Dean.

'What did his righteous holiness have to say about publishing the book then?'
The professor flinched. He was very fond of Amelia, but sometimes made to cringe at the way she referred to senior members of the church and the university.

'You're not a student any more darling. You might show some respect.'
Amelia moved towards her lover and reaching out her right hand pulled his head down onto her breasts,

'Like this do you mean?'

'There is a time and place Amelia. We've got to think how to deal with the Dean and his wretched Chapter.'
Amelia brought her left hand around between them and asked rather archly,

'What about this then?' She placed a large brown paper envelope on his desk and said,

'Open it lover boy.'
When Edward Clarke slit open the package, out tumbled two hundred or more pages of exact copies of Ned Scrivener's work, numbered and in order.

'I didn't let it go without scanning the whole thing. After all, what are computers for?'

'Darling you must have stayed up half the night to do this?'

'The whole night actually, both sides of the pages and now we have a PDF file of the complete shebang.'

'Good thinking Batman. Now we can work on it without anyone suspecting. Does anybody else know about this copy?'

'Not a soul, 'pon my honour yer worship.'

'Where's the file?'

'It's on my laptop at home.'

'The first place anyone would look.'

'I suppose so.'

'OK, copy it onto a memory stick and we can hide that anywhere.'

Edward looked more fondly than usual on his girlfriend's impish face,

'You are brilliant darling, nothing but brilliant. Now we'll print out another set of copies, one each, and we can work on them at our own pace.

Diana Clarke was surprised to find her usually errant husband seated at his desk at home in his own study on her return from yet another choir practice. Edward had his doubts about the existence of this choir. It was, he suspected, practice of a more horizontal kind.

'Cup of tea?' she asked.

'Mmm please,' was the pleasant response.

When she brought in the tea and a piece of marmite toast, she asked,

'Is that the old book back again?'

'Well sort of; it's a copy but nobody must know, it's a secret.'

'Copyright issues?'

'Exactly. Dr Gillies and I need to work on the text while the legal side is being sorted. We can't have the Cathedral lot publishing before us.'

'Of course not, that would be...a shame'

'...disastrous.' They both laughed knowing full well what each other meant. Professor Clarke had made his reputation and a good deal of money from publishing old manuscripts in popular styles. I fact their present house had been bought entirely from the royalties of his last book on the four mistresses of the Lord Lieutenant of

Hampshire in 1781 entitled,   *'Unruly in Beaulieu'*   from
which had emerged a subsequent TV series.

'So, another bodice ripper from the olden days?'
Diana was genuinely interested in her husband's work
when it was not an excuse for more of his meanderings.
She knew that he was an authentic scholar and a very
clever one. His contemporaries who criticised his
'popular' approach were jealous and they knew it.

'No, not quite as saleable as that yet, but an
interesting start,' said Edward.

§

Simon and his wife and my own landlady have prepared
a modest feast to celebrate my good fortune. The news of
my small triumph among my fellow scribes had soon
passed to my neighbours. So seldom had any craftsman
in this part of Firenze had their work publicly endorsed
in this way, (particularly by an illiterate pope,) that it was
an excellent excuse for some carousing. After the meal we
all had our cups in our hands and wandered into the
street.

Unfortunately, Matthias and his band of followers were
also walking past at the same time. There was no little
shouting and pushing until Simon Martial not knowing
who anyone was, but being very used to brawling at close
quarters, knocked Matthias down with his fist and drew
his dagger out in self defence as the other students closed
in on him. Fortunately I was able to shout out to them in
the local patois that Isabetta had been teaching me, that
he was a friend and they were to calm down. As most of
Matthias' group were not too fond of him and clearly
stayed in his presence only hoping for free wine, peace

was soon restored. Matthias however now lost his temper completely and challenged me as the host, to a duel. Some laughter accompanied this challenge. Matthias' own friends reminded him that duelling was illegal, and that it was only acceptable between aristocrats if at all. One student Johannes of Amsterdam shouted.

'What about a contest? A test of skill? Who throws a knife the best?'

Matthias spurned the idea of knife throwing. He had practised with a crossbow for many years and had heard that I was interested in archery.

'Can Ned Scrivener use a crossbow?' he challenged. I felt obliged to answer.

'I can respond Matthias to a match with a real bow,' I smiled, and he agreed. I knew that he believed that nothing was as effective as the new crossbow which was a machine and therefore superior. What he did not know was that the power of the longbow is in the archer's pull.

'At what distance do you agree to hold the contest?' I asked. At this, Mattias looked quite sly. The most effective range for accuracy with the crossbow was 100 paces.

'I challenge Ned to shoot at...' then he paused, '150 paces.' the crowd gave a massed sigh. Simon looked towards me and winked. We had been practicing at 250 paces with one another for nearly two years now and that had been the requirement for practice in almost every English village for the last 100 years.

I had a secret weapon.

Both sides agreed to meet and establish the rules of the contest within two days. Simon took me aside and came up with a plan that he had already worked out before the challenge. He said he had seen this all coming for weeks and had been thinking how it should be arranged.

The field must be set up exactly as Matthias had determined in all respects. The two targets would be at 150 paces and painted with the regular concentric circles of a standard mark, with a gold centre for the bulls eye about the size of a man's fist.

The next Sunday afternoon Matthias and his supporters and a surprising number of others, whom I did not know, gathered at the archer's field. I had my own longbow and a sheaf of 30 long arrows at my back. Simon and a friend of Matthias' had set two targets at 150 paces. Matthias had a shiny looking crossbow which shot bolts with hard metal points but the bolts were shorter than an English arrow.

We were each allowed one free shot before the competition began in earnest. Matthias shot first and hit his target about two inches above the bull. My trial shot was in the bull as it was the sort of practice I had been doing for some years. After that the real battle began.

We each now had one minute to fire as many arrows as we liked. Matthias started to shoot and he hit his bull again. He now had to reload a new bolt and wind back the string. In the meantime I shot three arrows into my bull. It was easy to take a new arrow from the quiver at my back and shoot in one easy movement. I could usually fire ten to twelve arrows in a minute. Something, I think that had not occurred to Matthias. His second shot after taking half a minute to reload, was in the bull once more. He was certainly an expert with the crossbow. I fired three more arrows all into the gold at the centre. Then suddenly to the surprise of everyone, a ripe melon appeared about ten feet behind my target and just enough above it to be seen. It was too much of a temptation and I fired a seventh arrow before the minute was counted. It split the melon into many pieces and little Isabetta stepped to the side to show that she had placed it on her head, and that she was completely unafraid. The gathering raised a huge cheer and began to laugh. I ran over to Matthias as his third shot also hit the bulls eye, and congratulated him, as he could not have done better with a crossbow.

It seems that Simon, remembering the story of Wilhelm Tell, had persuaded Isabetta to hide behind my target with the melon.

The contest had been hailed as a tie.

Chapter Eleven

I have become quite an eager citizen here in Firenze. I like the people and I especially love the buildings. The city is entirely surrounded by high walls with houses built into them. Many of the inhabitants can read and write. Some are writing books which challenge our thinking, especially about the infallibility of the pope and the place of the clergy in daily life. There is much trade from other parts of Europe and the four bridges across the Arno are likely to overflow with the traffic from north and south. I love the open piazzas which are so different from our cities at home. The Piazza della Signoria, the Piazza del Duomo and many others where people parade in the evenings and where many processions are held. The weather makes for the kind of outdoor life that we seldom see in England except on one or two days of summer.

Why am I writing at all in such a happy way? I have become such a sinner. But when I am so blessed with my life it is impossible to think of sin. I confine my life story only to this journal, which is locked at all times and written in English which very few people here can read. The plain truth is that I am in love.

The night after the archery contest, Isabetta who normally sleeps in bed with her grandmother, came into my room after darkness had fallen and came to lie beside me. She told me that she had attained her eighteenth year. I have said it is no sin to be tempted, and I was sorely tempted that night. Isabetta put her arms around me and offered herself in all her faithful innocence to me. At first, thinking of my own Emily whom I had now not seen for over a year, I resisted the temptation to true fornication.

Isabetta is a most pure and loving young woman with no experience of the world. She consented for two nights just to lie with me and for us to kiss one another. In the morning when we broke our fast, it was quite evident that Lucia had conspired with her and willingly let her sleep out of her bed. When I caught grandmother Lucia's eye and her wicked grin each morning I felt such pressure to play the part that I was clearly invited to perform, that I finally broke down. On the third morning I could envision nothing else in my mind all day long except that I would make love to sweet Isabetta that night, even against my strong beliefs. This time all caution was lost. I had never in my life before allowed the Devil to take charge of my desires. The feeling was not at all like hell but as I had imagined heaven to be. It was even more loving and perfect than when I had married Emily. My pupil became my companion at last. I had not realised all these weeks that I had been falling in love with her. I knew that it was wrong but it felt so right.

From now on we will be considered as husband and wife in Firenze, even though without the blessings of clergy.

Isabetta had been looking after me already, doing my washing and cleaning my room. But now it had become her room as well, she began to bring in flowers and a couple of small tapestries which she had been given to hang on the wall. She put her spare clothes into the coffer beneath the window, and made me sweetmeats and special soup on most days. I gave her a small dress allowance for herself which pleased her immensely. Of course her English improved every day from our most private conversations. My understanding of local Italian became more and more useful as well.

For the last week I have been torn between ecstasy and bliss, or in terror of losing my immortal soul.

Now I have come up with a plan. I sought out a priest nearby in a small church who takes regular confessions. I have also ascertained through friends, that he speaks no English. I went into the church after vespers and into the confessional. I knelt and in Latin I asked for my confession to be heard. The kindly priest agreed and I confessed my sins, including my fornication, in English. When I had finished he blessed me and gave me to say one dozen hail Marys.

I felt somehow relieved, as God seeth all of course, but my sin is now officially forgiven by the church.

§

'The cunning old bugger!'
Amelia looked up from her reading of the printed copy and laughed out loud and long. This was the stuff of social history that nobody taught you, she thought. We think we know all about the hypocrisy of bishops and kings and here is a humble low born serf showing us all a trick or two from the fourteenth century.

She called Professor Clarke on her smart phone. It was nine o'clock in the evening and she had been idly looking through the journal constantly trying to work out an angle for a modern version.

'Edward, have you got as far as our Ned having it off with Isabetta and then going to confession?'

'Hi Amelia, yes I read that bit last night, what's your take on it?'

'Well I think he is a crafty sod getting shriven by a priest who doesn't speak English. Is there anything like that in other pieces of contemporary literature?'

'Not really from such a humble chap, there are lots of confessions by saints and kings.'

'That was my thought. You expect the nobility to be manipulative of church and state but not some simple soul from the wilds of Hampshire. This is over 100 years before Machiavelli.'

'We'll read on then and see how he turns out?'

'OK; night love.'

Edward had not really seen the implication of the confession in the same way as Amelia had. But he began to see a possible angle to make their proposed book more commercial.

§

It is Christmastide tomorrow and many months since I recorded my thoughts in here. I am longing for the icy cold and snow of home. I wonder about Emily and little Justin, how they are faring. My homesickness hurts at times like a stomach colic.
My life with Isabetta is near perfection. Her family has accepted me completely as one of their own. She is a lovely girl and now with child and so looks more beautiful

every day. The unpleasantness with Matthias has gone completely. He has been given more responsibility in the scriptorium and has no reason to be envious of me any more.

I have been thinking about how I might make men do actions for me without them knowing what is happening. This is difficult to explain even unto myself. However, I have noted in the past how, if I am kind and generous with a person it hath more effect than being angry or chiding. This will happen in the ordinary way of things. But if I am anxious for a man to submit to my will, I can effect this by the same means. It is as if a kind word to a person creates a sort of debt which will be repaid later.

I believe that this is a God given gift to enable us to be at one with our fellow men. I have observed bishops and other senior priests to work in this way whether by design or by natural skill.

Meanwhile, I must attend to my first duty which has become to copy out texts from other scriptoria in different parts of Italy.

I have become quite expert in reading the old and new texts and translating the writing style into our new Florentine Carolingian. Many of my own copies have been sent to the Vatican in Rome.

Our monastery is Benedictine and so those scribes who are monks have to keep to their vows of silence. It is entertaining though to see how expertly they countermand their vows by an abundant use of sign language. There is even a list of permitted sign language set down by Saint Benedict himself many years agon. I have been shown the list by a monk Brother Bernardo, with whom I have become quite friendly. The manual has every sign of being written in the beginning by scribes at

Canterbury. It gives instructions as follows.

'Would you like some wine?' Use two fingers to simulate opening the tap of a cask.

'Pass the butter.' Stroke with three fingers on the inside of your hand.' Brother Nardo, as I now call him tells me that there are 127 signs listed. Of course our Benedictines have also many local signs that they have developed which are not listed, such as tapping the side of their head to say 'That man is an idiot.' Some of the monks are so adept at sign language that it is clear that they often prefer to use it rather than to speak.

Signor Poggio this morning asked me if I would be pleased to accompany him to Rome next week to the Vatican library. He has had an invitation from the senior librarian there, to discuss the large number of books which are being required nowadays. I agreed with some spirit and asked if I might bring Isabetta along to enlarge her experience of the world. He agreed gladly and suggested we give her a particular task to help explain her presence. I said what about laundry maid, and he considered that an excellent ruse.
We will be going by horse and carriage and not walking, the pinnacle of luxury. Simon Martial asked to be included as our guard to which Poggio was eager to accept. There was no room in the carriage, but Simon said he preferred to ride his own horse. He left his wife behind as she expressed no interest in seeing Rome.

When the day of our departure arrived, both Simon and I hid our longbows and sheaves of 50 arrows each in the bottom of the carriage.

We had hardly been on the journey for two days when a

band of vagabonds stopped us in the road and demanded our money and jewels. The leader was a very imposing figure tall and burly with an equally strong-looking lieutenant. They both wore swords. Signor Poggio forthwith gave way and loudly ordered myself and Simon to pull out the jewelry chest at the bottom of the carriage. Knowing full well that there was no jewelry box we both pretended to search inside the carriage. My amazing Isabetta climbed down and said that she needed to answer a call of nature. She diverted the two leaders of the band by squatting on the side of the road just within sight. Meanwhile Simon and I together produced our longbows and fitted arrows speedily. It was to our astonishment that we could not even make the ruffians look at us, they were so intent on watching Isabetta. She in turn, gave them some extremely frank views of her slender body. When together Simon and I stood up with our bows drawn and arrows pointing at the two leaders, it was a surprise to the whole gang. Simon did not hesitate but sent an arrow into the heart of the main robber. One second later, taking courage from his example I shot the second attacker in the neck. At this, the rest of the gang ran away. There were five of them. We soon gathered our wits again and all praised Isabetta for her quick thinking. Signor Poggio was so pleased with all of us that he immediately gave Simon, Isabetta and me a florin each. We continued quickly, without giving the thieves a Christian burial. We lay them together by the side of the road as a warning to other gangs. My legs were trembling all this time and my hands shaking. This was the first man I had ever killed.

Isabetta sat very close to me and held me tight until the shaking ceased, as we continued on to the nearest village which was Asciano. There was no accommodation to be had there, but some of the villagers told us of a religious house nearby. Then a few miles further south we came to a conspicuous red brick Benedictine monastery, Monte Oliveto Maggiore. The monks took us in on hearing our tale and said that the gang had been causing havoc in the neighbourhood stealing and murdering. We were made very welcome and given their best guest lodgings.

That night as I lay under linen sheets on a full straw mattress, I could not stop shaking. I did not sleep for many hours and when I awoke I was alternately hot and cold. I constantly saw the image of the robber with my arrow through his neck. When Isabetta came to bring me some break fast, I was shivering still and unable to eat anything. Master Poggio came to see me and declared that I was disturbed by the devilish spirits of the dead man. Only faith would heal me. I was to stay in bed while the monks prayed for my soul and my recovery. He and the others would make themselves useful around the monastery and wait for me.

Meanwhile I slept and I had a dream. I can recall it well. I dreamt I was back in Winchester but the weather was hot and sunny like Firenze. I was working on a difficult manuscript which was to be written on very rough canvas, almost impossible to use with an ordinary quill pen; when Lord Rollo FitzStephen came up behind me and whispered menacingly for me to give him the money. I turned and saw that he had an arrow through his neck. Emily was then pulling me away from Rollo and crying piteously. She was shouting, 'Come home, come home, we need you.' As I dreamed on, Giles riding Providence arrived and challenged Lord Rollo with a sword.

I woke feeling light-headed and angry, for I thought I could easily interpret such a dream. Yet any meaning did not become clear to me as time passed.

§

Dr Amelia Gillies typed expertly on her laptop, the one
she used exclusively for her own work. It was not
connected to the internet or even a network in college.
She was paranoid about other people stealing her ideas
and kept this private and personal computer at home at
all times. She needed to type her reactions and ideas as
she read the diary and so for her, reading and reactive
writing always went together.

She had handed Edward Clarke the memory stick where
she had stored the scanned pages of the Scrivener to look
after, as well as the 200 or so printed sheets. However, she
retained the original scanned copy and was writing her
own notes and ideas for the proposed book continuously
as she read through Ned Scrivener's manuscript. She had
already determined what her 'take' on the journal would
be. It seemed obvious to her that it was to be an example
of the psychology of a medieval man. She had quickly
cottoned on to the notion that Ned was an intellectual
and a thinker in spite of his limited education. His
insights and his commentaries went far further than the
usual monastic education of those days.

Now this dream of his was a gift.

There were also the stories of Emily and Isabetta, as well
as Perreta the Alpine guide, all strong women who made
decisions and took actions without the restrictions laid on
them by men. She was also surprised to find that many of
the scribes and illuminators were women. She had always
assumed that they were men. So in her own mind the
stage was set for a treatise on medieval psychology and
early feminism. She did not think that her lover Edward
would appreciate her ideas and so she had no intention

of sharing them.

Chapter Twelve

When our party set out towards Rome again, we found that once on the main highway we were being overtaken by pilgrims of many nations. All of them travelled in groups of not fewer than twelve for mutual protection. The pilgrims were happy to talk of their plans and of their experiences. Most were from northern Italy travelling to Rome and on to ports such as Taranto or Otranto. There they planned to take ships further east and to the Holy Land.

I admired the pilgrims for their fortitude. No-one knows better than I the difficulties of travelling on foot across Europe. It is their motives that I do not understand. If God is everywhere and sees us at all times, where is the merit in visiting places where his saints and his only son dwelt? Surely, if one spent a decent life wherever one lived, it would be as valuable to God as any pilgrimage? I believe that most pilgrims were merely curious about the world and wanted an excuse to travel.

Some of the pilgrim's stories did speak of miracles at shrines such as St Cataldus at Taranto. Pilgrims had been healed of lameness or even blindness. But there were so few that it could have been luck. Also, who knows what is in men's hearts when they tell these tales? Hope or bragging?

The practical advice from pilgrim travellers was of greatest value. Many listed the inns which were welcoming or which were ill-disposed. The particular care of one's feet, I was told, was to soak them in mild vinegar and to rub with garlic. This has proved most agreeable.

I now believe that the pilgrims from England start out with holy ideas but after a few weeks they become more interested in the journey itself and the companionship along the way. When I asked which holy places they recall the most, they will always refer to the wine and beer or the sights, or the good time they had in one town or another. A number of the pilgrims have picked up women on the way. As have some of the women pilgrims also gathered men unto themselves. I was told that a small number have just stopped in certain towns or villages, obtained work and a new family. This is almost certainly due to the ravages of the population five and twenty years ago. There is still a shortage of experienced middle-aged men and women everywhere since that abomination called the Black Death.

Nine days after our start we have reached the holy city of Rome. I cannot begin to describe Rome. Unless you have been here it is impossible to imagine. I recall when I first admired Winchester cathedral, it was the largest object I had ever seen. Well, Rome seems to be full of buildings at least double the size of our little cathedral at home. It makes me wonder what heaven must be like. If man has built this city what has God built in heaven ?

The Vatican is a city inside a city. The walls are too high

for anyone to climb. But our little party was expected and we were welcomed in. First we were told where we would be staying. It is in a small albergo, I think owned by the Vatican and outside its walls. We have all, even Isabetta, been given small metal badges to show that we are guests of the pope. Thus we may easily come and go to the Vatican library.

The next day Master Poggio took me with him to meet the librarian Cardinal Mosto. He was an imposing man who seemed to be holding himself as too important to be in charge of a mere library. However, he was gracious and showed us through the several rooms packed with scrolls which were very impressive. Mosto explained that there were as many books and scrolls in Avignon where the anti-pope resided. One day, he said, he prayed that the two libraries would come together; but to me this one in itself was quite enough. He asked me how many manuscripts had I copied and was surprised at the number. When he discovered that I could draw and illuminate as well as write in Latin, French, Greek and English, Cardinal Mosto looked particularly grave and took my hands in his very soft ones and blessed them saying he had use for my skills here in Rome. He held my hands for what I would describe as too long, but he is a cardinal and I am but a humble serf.

 He then threw his scarlet cloak around me and taking me as a bird under his wing, guided me further round the collection, explaining each to me that they were from Paris or Sweden and even Esztergon in Hungary. After a while I found myself in Cardinal Mosto's private quarters. He bade me to sit, and called a servant to bring wine and some fruit. There was no sign of master Poggio. After we had both drunk two gasses of wine, the Cardinal commented on how strong I was and asked if I took regular exercise. I said indeed I did and told him about myself and Simon and how we both practised our archery at least once a week. I then told him the tale of how we killed the two robbers. He became seemingly quite excited by the story, and made me tell it to him twice.

After that, I thought it wise to say that my master Signor Poggio was expecting me. I thanked the Cardinal and hoped to meet again and left. It was a tricky maze to find my way out. The effect of the wine was strong and I stumbled once or twice, but my badge meant that various servants hastened to show me how to proceed.

It is hard for a humble scribe to resist the temptations put forward by senior clergy, and I am well aware of some of the unnatural acts which low born men and women are often forced to perform. I hope in God's name that I did the right thing, but as I have written before, it is no sin to be tempted.

§

'I must say this guy's journal seems to have everything!' exclaimed Edward to Diana. He put down his empty mug on the desk where he worked at home. There were already coffee rings on the printed out pages of the journal.

'Why what's happened now?' asked his wife.

'So far, murder and seduction to sodomy!' said the professor in a smug tone.

'What actual, you know, doing it?'

'No, but he took a wise decision to escape from it in the Vatican library of all places.'

'Give it here, let's have a look,' said Diana and laughingly Edward handed over the scanned copy.

'I can't read this it's all in ancient script.'

'Of course darling, but if you work at it you can read it. It is in English of a sort.'

'You read it to me then.'

The professor was glad to read aloud the last couple of pages that he had been studying closely.

'Have you decided how to play your own treatise about this one yet?' asked his wife.

'Not at all. At the moment I am too deeply engaged in the story, but I tell you what.'

'What?'

'I think we should travel to Florence and maybe Rome ourselves and get a feel for it.'

'Darling now you're talking! I'll have to get a whole new outfit.'

'Hang on, I didn't mean right away, just that we might go sometime.'

'But we will go right?'

'In the long vac., and we'll go to both.'

§

I was glad to get back to the albergo and to my beautiful Isabetta. The sudden experiences of Rome and of meeting important people had given me a megrim.

I have lain abed for a week now and feeling so low that Isabetta treated me with an infusion of hypericum perforatum, which we call St John's wort. This has helped, also with prayers from Simon and master Poggio. I feel so foolish but Isabetta is so strong and practical that she has convinced me that I had been ill for some time and too much work and novelty has brought on this distemper. Master Poggio assures me that the Cardinal librarian is very impressed with my wit and has also sent six bottles of his best red wine. I find that I cannot even consider drinking wine at the moment, but I am sure it will help to build my strength as I improve. Cardinal Mosto has kindly lent me a small but valuable Arabic scroll with details of herbal remedies. He has attached his own translation which is most charitable of him. I am impressed with such knowledge and it has made me determined to add Arabic to my own store of languages. Isabetta scolds me for even thinking of such exertions, which she says will close my pores and stop the work of the hypericum.

***

It is three months agon since I last wrote and much has happened which surprises us all. Firstly, I have persevered with the Arabic language and seem to have a gift for these things. In another three months I expect to be able to translate simple instructions in that language. The Mussulman religion and philosophy is of great interest to me but it is unpopular to speak too well of these things in Rome especially in the Vatican. More important than this is that I have been appointed a papal messenger at a salary which taketh my breath away. I have rented a modest house not too far from the Vatican and am set up almost as a signore. Cardinal Mosto has proved to be a wonderful friend. I know full well that he has ladylike tendencies, but he he is genuinely kind-hearted and interested in my career. We understand one another and there is no question of any kind of sin between us. He has given me new confidence in my abilities and my future.

Isabetta is now near her time with the new child. She is healthy and beautiful. I shall ask the pope to dissolve my marriage with Emily, much as I still love her, but I am Isabetta's husband now. I am also responsible for her Grandmother Lucia who lives with us in my new house. She is in charge of the servants and the cooking and we are fortunate to have her. Never in my whole life did I imagine that I would own a house and servants. This could not have happened in England I am sure.

Using my growing knowledge of Arabic, I am now studying medicine. It seems that the Musselmen are famous for their knowledge of the humours, black bile, yellow bile, blood and phlegm. They are also skilled in the many herbs once grown by the ancient Greeks. I am allowed, nay encouraged, to study any of the manuscripts in the library providing that I copy any that I read. This is in contrast to England where most scriveners can copy, but not necessarily read all the languages.

Cardinal Mosto tells me that the Pope is ill with a fever and a lingering cough with a chest pain. He is in great distress. I am searching the Arabic and other scrolls for any information that might help His Holiness. Roger Frugard of Palma has a number of helpful pages of illuminated advice. There is also The Canon of Medicine which is widely read in monasteries. I have suggested St Paul's Potion to the Cardinal. This is a complex mixture of liquorice, sage, willow, roses, fennel, cinnamon, pepper, ginger, cloves and a few more herbs. The Cardinal has suggested that I search the Vatican garden myself and make up the potion and he will take it to him. After a pleasant half hour searching in the sunny garden, I finally discovered the well-hidden herb plot which had evidently been neglected for a season. It had been planted in a square pattern by someone who knew what to do and each small quadrate contained a herb. The little plots were still well-labelled. There must have been a hundred. After some judicious weeding I found almost all the plants I needed. I took two hours mixing and completing the St Paul's Potion. Then took it at once to Cardinal Mosto. Isabetta, who is already skilled in these things, having learned from her grandmother as a child, has also made up a soothing cordial. This too has been taken to Pope Boniface IX His Holiness himself.

Chapter 13

Dr Amelia Gillies was on her third reading of the journal, or Ned's diary as she had come to refer to it. She was still excited by the whole thing. To be fair, her interest was entirely academic, with no thought of money although with a big dollop of ambition. She was a comprehensive school girl from Banbury, an only child, who had gained a scholarship to St Catherine's Oxford and a first in medieval history. Her parents were a proud middle-class couple. Her father a garden designer and her mother a midwife. They were both near retirement nowadays and spent their long summers exploring the canals of England and Wales.

She had telephoned her parents after her first reading of the diary and explained to them how unusual and important it was. Neither of them could quite understand her enthusiasm but were both delighted that their clever daughter was doing well. Her doctorate was completed at Winchester under (in all senses of the word) Professor Edward Clarke.

Apart from the professor, Amelia had a serious boyfriend of her own age who was a junior editor in a small publishing house, Harrington's of Reading. The firm specialised in local history mostly in the south of

England. They liked to publish countryside guides, wartime tales from Alton, Basingstoke etc. and sea stories from the Hampshire and Sussex coasts. His name was Robert Simms and they had met at Oxford when he was studying English literature.

Edward Clarke knew nothing of Robert Simms, but Robert knew all about Edward and Amelia's relationship. He was quite relaxed about it all because he claimed to have a laid back personality. He loved Amelia but he was glad she had this influential senior academic at her beck and call.

One day, he thought, it would all pay off and he would have a famous wife or partner. They would both earn pots of money and probably live in France or Spain. In fact he was a nice young man of 27 whom Amelia still adored, but who had not emotionally grown past the age of eighteen.

Amelia could not wait to show Robert her copy of Ned's diary and drove her second-hand Ford Kia to Robert's flat in the east of Reading the next Saturday morning. His first reaction was,

'We couldn't possibly publish this at Harrington's sweetheart.'

'I understand that darling, I just wanted to share it with you. It's remarkable you realise?'

'If you say so, have you got a translation of it I could look at?'

'No, it would take weeks, can't you read this script? Well, take this memory stick with the whole thing on and keep it safe for me.'

Robert answered by taking her in his arms and murmuring there were other activities he would prefer.

On Amelia's return after the weekend there was a

message on her answerphone to ring Tristan Smallwood the archivist at the cathedral office. He answered at once.

'Ah you are Professor Clarke's assistant I understand?'

'Yes I am. What can I do for you?'

'It is rather, what I can do for you Dr Gillies. Could you come and see me here at the cathedral offices?'

'Yes of course, when?'

'Anytime today.'

'How about ten o'clock?'

At ten Amelia arrived at Smallwood's tiny compartment in the overcrowded office, and was offered a cup of Nescafe. The archivist spoke,

'The thing is Dr Gillies, the Dean and Chapter would like to offer you a job to do with the recent discovery of the medieval journal which I had to reclaim from you the other morning.'

'Really, what sort of job?'
Amelia made round eyes at Mr Smallwood and even flirted a little.

'We thought we might have been a little unfair to you, a bit quick to judge, and we would like to make it up to you. Would you translate and edit the journal as a professional historian, for reprinting and sale in the Cathedral shop? We will of course offer a professional fee. I am not so naïve, in this digital age, to think that you did not make a copy of the book before I seized it, correct?'

§

I waited anxiously for any report of the Pope's condition.

After 24 hours I was summoned by a servant to the chambers of Cardinal Mosto. When I was ushered in he looked happy and came forward to greet me with both hands, as was his manner when feeling generous.

'My boy,' he said, 'His Holiness is much better already. I think we have great hopes. To begin with his pain has eased, and between you and me I am not at all convinced that the prayers of all the cardinals are responsible, as we have been praying for a week now. It is since your potion that his recovery has started.'
I immediately knelt for a blessing as I knew full well that is what Mosto most liked.

Two days later, I was sent for again by the cardinal. This time he seemed overjoyed.

'His Holiness would like to see you. He is feeling so much better and is very aware that it is thanks to you. Tonight at six of the clock, come properly dressed to my chambers here and I will take you in.'

I bowed and retired shaking with nervousness and anticipation. I had never seen the Pope since his brief visit to our scriptorium in Firenze. Not many laymen were ever granted an audience, and as far as I knew never a humble serf from England.
At six o'clock I presented myself in my best clothes and followed the cardinal down several corridors to what I realised were the Pope's own private quarters. We were ushered in by two papal guards who both checked that I had no weapons. I then saw his holiness sitting up in bed in a brocaded gown. He looked pale but well and held out his hand for me to kiss. Cardinal Mosto introduced me as Ned the English Scrivener who had made the St Paul's potion.

'I am very thankful to you Englishman for

researching my cure and for making it up yourself. I am truly grateful. I believe that you have saved my life. Now I want to know how can I reward you? Cardinal Mosto speaks very highly of your work and your wit and skills.' I was overcome with shyness, but not so much that I could not speak my heart's desire.

'Your Holiness,' I spoke and sank on one knee as I assumed was expected, 'I would beg an annulment of my marriage to Emily in England, as I am now promised to an Italian lady from Firenze.'

'Dear Ned, my son, consider it so. Mosto will see to the details, but I wish to do you more honour than this from a heartfelt gratitude. We have an empty castle in Tuscany whose owner has died leaving it in our gift. I would be pleased if you accepted it and the title and monies which go with it.'

On hearing this I nearly swooned but managed to kiss His Holiness' hand and stutter how grateful I was and so pleased that he had recovered. After a few more niceties the cardinal signalled for us to withdraw and we left the chamber. My head was spinning with wonder at what the details might be about the gift.

It turns out that the castle is the Castello Monte Ariggio only a few leagues from Firenze. I am now Prince Ariggio, which is the title that goes with the castle, also ten farms which surround the castle nearby in Tuscany and three apartment buildings in Rome. All of which provide what is to me an enormous income, so much that I cannot even conceive it.

I rushed to tell my Isabetta that she was now to be a principessa when we shall be married. As soon as I can be spared I shall take her to look at our castle. My good fortune will tempt me into becoming arrogant unless I am severe with myself. Pride goeth before a fall. When we get back to Firenze, what will Mathias think? Even more vital, what will he do?

It was arranged for me to return to Firenze immediately and Cardinal Mosto assured me that with my new status all doors would be opened to me. He would deal with my annulment and send a message confirming it to the Bishop of Winchester in the next ship to England.

Isabetta and I travelled home in a carriage that was the first thing I bought with my new found wealth.

I was then introduced to the complexities of banking and bills of exchange within the newly formed Medici bank in Firenze by my master Poggio Bracciolini, who also released me from my post at once. He helped me to arrange the collection of my rents from the farms and the properties in Rome. All this unaccustomed business made my head spin but I pretended to understand it all, hoping that it would come to me eventually.

A week after our arrival home We were awakened early in the morning by a loud knocking on the door. I answered and found myself pushed inside by four men armed with cudgels. Lucia screamed and this brought Isabetta to the room. I was held by three of the men while the fourth set about me with his weapon. I realised by his angry outbursts that it was Mathias.

'Take this *Prince!* You slimy foreign toad!' was just one of his cries that I remember. Quick thinking Isabetta slipped outside and ran to my friend Simon's home only a few yards away. She brought him back with his sword, but by this time, I was unconscious and the men were gone. They lifted me up and put me in my own bed. It was an hour or more they tell me, before I came to. I was bruised all over and had a large bump on the side of my head which had been the worst blow.

Forthwith I decided to ask Simon to become our bodyguard and to hire half a dozen trustworthy men to assist him. I blamed myself for not having thought of this earlier. But now I began to realise how much my life was going to change and how I might protect my family by using some of this vast wealth that I had so suddenly received. I also had a unforeseen longing to see England again; to put some distance between ourselves and any trouble in Italy. We could do with some leisure time to help us to stop one kind of life and to become used to another. In preparation for this, I allowed my short hair to grow in the modern Italian fashion and I cultivated a small aristocratic beard as a disguise. With my new fine clothes I had no doubt that no-one in England would recognise me.

After two weeks Simon had become my very own bailiff and factotum. He had sought out and hired several servants and men-at-arms, all equipped with horses. The sum involved was paltry compared with my income. The banker Giovani di Bicci de' Medici was only too keen to arrange letters of credit with a moneylender in Winchester. This will be ready with cash after 21 days, which is about the time it will take to sail from Genoa to Southampton. I pray for good weather and a following wind. I shall take four servants and four men-at-arms. We go by our own coach to Genoa. I shall leave it to be driven back to my castle and buy another when we reach England.

I heard nor saw anything more of Mathias. I assume he

had taken fright and left Firenze.

I began to worry about who would look after my castle and take the rents while we are in England until Simon suggested that I send for Ralf and offer him the job. I asked Simon to find him for me in Milano if he was still there. Accordingly, he took two good horses and rode full speed to find his friend. In three days they were back. Ralf had a wife and daughter and his own horse. He had been working as a mercenary soldier for a minor nobleman, but Simon easily persuaded him that he would be much better off with us and be paid top rate as my Marshal. I was overjoyed to see my old friend. Simon took another day to take him to Castello Monte Ariggio and to settle in. By the time he returned to our home in Firenze we were ready to leave. In the meantime, I had taken the advice of my banker Giovanni di Bicci to purchase 100 rolls of the best silken cloth. As he said, what is the purpose of taking a trading ship to England without trading?

My worries now were beginning to make me think of the saying of Our Lord, *"Again I tell you, it is easier for a camel to go through the eye of a needle than for someone who is rich to enter the kingdom of God."* It is almost impossible not to become a worshipper of mammon when you have the responsibility of money.

Isabetta was coming near to her time and I had to accept that our child would likely to be borne on board the vessel. So I hired a midwife who was a friend of Isabetta's grandmother Lucia to accompany us. I wanted Simon to come as a sort of bodyguard and to give him a chance to see England again. He left his wife Lisa with many tears on her part, but I could tell that he was excited.

Chapter 14

When Professor Clarke heard from Amelia the next day telling him about the offer of the Dean to translate the journal, he was hurt rather than angry. He had supposed that he would be the person to whom they would turn. Then it occurred to him that it was flattering that they should choose the pupil that he had trained and perhaps there would be a better opportunity coming up soon. After all there was going to be little financial gain from producing a local book sold only in the cathedral shop.

Tristan Smallwood and Dean Brian Woodward were chuckling together in the cathedral office.

'So she fell for it did she?'

'Hook, line and sinker Dean.'

'It was a good idea, Professor Clarke would never have agreed to it, I think he is much too canny. We retain the copyright ourselves, once it's in the shop,' said the Dean rubbing his hands.

'Then can we can send the journal for Sothebys to sell and hope that The British Library or the Americans will come up trumps?' said Smallwood.

'I'll give Sir Quentin a ring.' said the Dean.

§

The ship looked exceedingly small to be taking us so far. Simon and I both remembered our trip from Dover to Calais as disastrous. However, this time we were honoured passengers and had snug sleeping quarters below decks. I made sure that Isabetta was comfortable with the midwife nearby. *Le Nostre Dame* was the name of our ship. The master who was English, was called Captain Dickon Forester. He was very experienced and had made this trip both ways more than 30 times. He was clearly anxious to be of service. He complimented me on my command of English which took me aback, as I had not yet thought of myself as a real Italian prince. It was a useful experience, as I then made sure that I had a slight Italian accent when speaking my own language, otherwise explanations were going to be too complex.

I thought of Colossians 3:9 *Do not lie to one another, seeing that you have put off the old self with its practices.* I was getting deeper into living a falsehood, would I regret it?

By the time I stopped thinking about myself we were two leagues off the coast in very calm weather and bound for Barcelona.

The arrival in the busy harbour of Barcelona was my and Isabetta's first sight of Spain. It seemed so much more foreign than either France or Italy especially as neither of us spoke the language. The ship stopped only for four hours to take on fresh water and fresh vegetables. So we had a short walk around the harbourside and came running back to the sound of a hunting horn blown by the mate to hurry us all aboard once again.

I think that our exertions yesterday have brought on my Isabetta's time. The midwife who is a strong but sometimes disagreeable woman has banned me from my wife's chamber or cabin. I know nothing of what is going on. The wind has increased as we proceed down the Spanish coast to Jebel Tariq which the ancients called the Pillars of Hercules and where we do not land as it is inhabited by fierce Musselmen. When we emerge into the Mare Tenebrosum, the captain has told me that we shall make for Cadiz which is also in Spain.

It has been four days since I wrote in this book. Meanwhile, the wind has proved very strong as soon as we passed the pillars of Hercules and turned north. Although it was only 65 miles to Cadiz we hardly moved against the storm. I believe it actually blew us backwards for the first day. We were all sick including the crew and I prevailed against the midwife to see my Isabetta who seemed unconcerned thanks be to God.
She gave birth in the night before last, before we arrived at Cadiz. We have a healthy boy which we will name Piero after the pope himself.
I write this in the calm haven of Cadiz which I was so relieved to enter. Here Captain Forester decreed that we might spend two nights to recover and to take in water and fresh food once again. Two of the crew who were brothers have deserted and the captain is trying to hire two replacements. I have checked on my cargo of silk and it is safe and dry.
After another rough crossing we called in at Vigo in northern Spain, evidence of what a large country it is. Today we are due in Southampton after 23 days.

§

Davy Lawson and his friend Jim Morgan were playing in the cathedral roof again. This time they had climbed into their favourite spot completely unobserved.

'Do you think we might find another of those books Davy?' asked Jim.

'I doubt it, that one was very rare according to my Dad.'

'Rare and valuable?'

'Yeah worth millions I believe.'

'Well it's an idea to have another look anyway.'

'OK, where do we start?'

'Let's go back to the pillar where we found it and work right round the roof.'

The boys crept back to the part of the support where the book had been concealed. They stuck their hands into every crevice they could see, as they worked their way clockwise around the roof-space. They found some very rusty nails and small shards of limestone. After half an hour they were both covered in dust and getting tired. They had not even gone a third of the way.

'Bugger this for a game of soldiers,' said Davy, 'Let's give it up for now and come back another day.'

'OK, but I reckon that we should get a reward for finding the book', grumbled Jim.

'Yeah, why don't we find the bishop or someone and make our claim?'

'Brilliant idea, but we'll need our dads to prove it was us.' Davy scratched on the nearest pillar with a bit of limestone to show how far they had come around.

The boys climbed down to the back of the choir and through the tiny access door that was their secret.

§

The sight of Southampton lifted all our hearts and the faint smoky smell of England was so welcome as to bring tears to my eyes. It was almost midday and many traders and longshoremen stood on the quayside to welcome us in. I had decided to wait a day or two before journeying on to Winchester. Captain Dickon had suggested a hostelry.

Isabetta, little Piero, Dominica, Simon and myself went ashore to find the place. We walked up to the magnificent Norman Bargate built over 200 years agon and still a fine edifice to welcome us. We came to the popular Red Lion Hostelry where Captain Forester had already sent a messenger to reserve us all rooms. I also arranged for my two other guards to stay in a bothy at the rear. I was just beginning to feel the power of status and money which was a fanciful state of mind compared to my previous life, but it was nevertheless easy to assume.

After an exceedingly comfortable night and an English breakfast consisting of bread, good English wine and some excellent fillets of smoked anchovy, Simon and I set out to explore the city.

It was a busy place with much trade of all kinds going on I had sent for my bales of silken cloth and soon found a merchant anxious to buy for a high price. Thus I had a considerable sum of English money to hand immediately. I paid Simon his wages straightaway in silver and hired a carriage and two strong horses, with the option to buy if they were satisfactory. I may have money now, but I was born a cunning serf not a poop-noddy.

We returned to the Red Lion pretty pleased with our day. Supper was ready but Isabetta and Dominica had not yet returned, so Simon and I summoned two mugs of ale while we waited. After an hour and they still had not returned I began to worry. After two hours Simon suggested we go to look for them in the town. Darkness had fallen and most of the stalls were shut. I sent one of my men to fetch the constable and the other I sent down towards the harbour. Simon and I looked along the high street but with no sign of them. What worried me was that neither of them spoke the sort of English dialect needed in Hampshire.

Beside which there was the baby. I knew Isabetta could feed him but who would feed Isabetta?

Chapter 15

Edward and Diana Clarke were planning their trip. Their two suitcases were open on the bed between them. Edward had long finished reading the journal which, although it was not written completely up to the end of Ned's life, went far enough to be intriguing.

'We must visit Florence and Rome.' urged Diana.

'But don't forget the Castello Monte Ariggio, we have to find that,' said the professor, 'and perhaps we should take Amelia along with us?'

'Over my dead body Edward.' Diana's eyes pierced her husband's from across the room.

'Just joking dear.'

'Dead body I said, I meant yours of course.'

'Oh something interesting happened this morning,' countered Edward changing the subject. 'That boy David Lawson and the friend of his Jim, came to see me before college. They wanted an introduction to the bishop to claim a reward.'

'What did you say to them ?'

'I said the bishop had nothing to do with it, but that I would reward them myself and what did they think would be fair. They had obviously thought about it and wanted fifty pounds between them. I asked if they would be happy with twenty and they agreed at once. So I coughed up straightaway, good value I thought.'

'Edward you really are a cheapskate sometimes.'

'Well, I haven't earned a penny out of it yet and now there is the expense of this junket around Italy.'

'I though you had a research grant for it?'

'It hasn't come through yet, I'm beginning to have my doubts about it.'

'Is that why you suggested Amelia? Is she better than you at getting grants out of people? Typical; I suppose she just lies down on some government office carpet opens her knees and money falls out of the sky.'

'Well – er...'

'I'm right aren't I? I knew it!' Diana slammed her case shut and stormed out of the room. In truth she didn't care one way or another, but it was a beautiful way to score off her silly husband.

§

Thank the Lord they have been found!
The following morning one of my men arrived with Dominica and my little family unharmed. It would seem that in the high street they had been threatened by two ruffians who then gave chase, but Dominica ducked into the doorway of a house and pulled my two in after her. The lady of the house, a good Hampshire woman, took them in and let them hide for several hours. After dark they were both too scared to go outside again, being strangers in the land. Their saviour could not understand a word they said, including Isabetta's English, which I fear must be almost a private tongue between the two of us. They stayed overnight and in the morning ventured forth just as one of my searchers was nearby. I am so

relieved. I gave my man a gold piece and sent another down to the kind woman who had befriended them. But I have decided to travel on to Winchester away from this undesirable port. Within two hours we were all riding in the carriage I had hired and in another two we had arrived at the cathedral close and being greeted by the bishop's servants outside the palace.

Everything looked so familiar and most of the faces were of old friends or the scribes. As Isabetta and I descended from our conveyance no-one recognised me. My fine clothes, long hair and pointed beard must have made it impossible. I was introduced to Bishop William as Prince Ariggio de Monte Ariggio, emissary from the pope. I had the coffer of books and scrolls carried into the palace and gave Simon and the others the rest of the day free.

The bishop's servants led us to the best rooms that they had prepared and Isabetta and I jumped on the huge bed and laughed like children. After a short while we were summoned into the bishop's private room, which I had never seen before. After a few compliments were exchanged the bishop praised my command of the English language. He asked,

'Have you visited England before, Prince Ariggio?' I replied with a question,

'I began life here in Hampshire. Do you not recognise me your grace?'
Bishop William looked puzzled and said that he did not.

'I am truly Ned Scrivener behind this beard as God is my witness.' I then knelt and kissed his hand as I had learned in the Vatican how senior churchmen love men to do this.

'I have the honour to present my lady Principessa Isabetta of Ariggio. I beckoned Isabetta forward and she made a knee well and put out her hand most prettily.

Bishop William said nothing , his mouth hung open until he came to himself eventually.

'Ned, an Italian prince? How so? I see now that it is you my boy. I have just received the annulment of your other marriage.'

Isabetta was then excused as she could hear the baby crying.

We conversed for about an hour as I told him of my adventures and my change of fortunes. I begged him not to reveal to anyone else who I was.

'I will try to do as you ask but I cannot tell a falsehood. Well, well, well, you saved the pope's life. That honour is not given to many,' he smiled and shook my hand for the third time.

I then asked what had become of young Lord FitzStephen.

'Fallen on hard times,' said the Bishop, 'crops failed for two seasons on his estate and Sir Rollo gambled much away. Perhaps you do not know, but your earlier wife Emily wasn't it? She became his mistress only a few months after you left. He has adopted your son as his own and intends to wed her I am told.'

I was relieved to hear this as the fate of Emily had been much on my mind. This truly was welcome news. I longed however to see young Justin my firstborn, who must be almost three by now and somehow to contrive to speak to Justin the bailiff and my old friend Giles the marshall.

Isabetta and I had a fine meal at the bishop's table and spent a quiet night in his guest room.

The following day I took Isabetta and two of my own horses and rode out dressed in all our best finery to Twyford and the FitzStephen estate. Simon accompanied us for some protection if necessary. I could see that some of the buildings were looking run down and many weeds grew in the fields in a way I have never seen before. We came across the marshall as we entered the main yard and stables. He bent a knee and greeted me as a very superior being.. I descended from my horse and leaving the others, I took Giles by the arm and walked him into the old stable where he usually sat. I spoke softly,

'Dear Giles, I may be an Italian prince now as you can see, but I am your devoted Ned Scrivener whom you taught French. I am come back to visit my friends but I do not want everyone to know it is me. Can you keep the secret?'

Of course Giles was amazed and at first disbelieving. However, it was not difficult to persuade him when I mentioned little known facts such as the small bow and arrows he had once made me. We spoke for several minutes, while the others waited patiently. I introduced them finally and we departed with Giles sworn to secrecy. He told me that Justin was in the city on some bailiff business and would no doubt be in the God Begot Inn. My own son Justin was with his mother indoors. By this time I was feeling too strange to risk seeing Emily even in disguise, and so we left and rode back to the bishop's palace.

Several days have passed since my last entry and I find I am tired of my own country and longing to return to Firenze. I would like to visit my castle and see if it will make a suitable home for us. It has been deserted for a year or more and will need some restoring I am sure. But mostly it is that my Italian friends are now more interesting and I have outgrown Winchester. Emily has settled, much to my surprise, with Sir Rollo, and obviously my eldest son is safe. Isabetta is uneasy in England. She does not like the food and does not speak the language as well as she had hoped.

I have decided that this part of England needs a bank in the manner of the Medicis. I believe that the port of Southampton would be a better situation for trade and so I have sent Simon to find a suitable plot of land for a building.

Yesterday, I discovered Justin the bailiff in his usual place in the God Begot Inn. I approached him in all my finery and asked who he was, and would he care to share a jug of ale with me. He told me his name and his status and accepted my offer gladly. I began to ask him about Winchester. While we talked I could see that he was looking at me in a strange way, but he answered my questions as I answered his about Italy. After a while he said,

'Pardon me Sir, but you speak English as well as an Englishman. Where did you learn our language?'
I answered,

'I learned right here in Hampshire, thanks to you.'
'What, what do you mean?' he cried.

'You found me yourself and took me to the FitzStephen's and made me a whipping boy. I owe everything to you Justin. I named my firstborn after you. Do you not recognise your boy Ned?'
At this, an expression of immense joy came over his face and he grasped me round the shoulders saying,

'I knew it! I knew it! I suspected it was you by your voice my lad, but I had no reason to believe it!'
We then had such a reunion for the next two hours while I told him everything about the past two and a half years. I also told him of my plans to open up a bank dealing with letters of credit in Southampton.

'Do you have enough money to start a bank?' he asked in amazement.

'More than enough.'

I was able to say without a lie. He promised faithfully to keep secret who I really was, but warned that it would inevitably be discovered before long. We parted with many compliments and vows of friendship.

Justin was right, two days later I was in Jewry Street dealing with old Abraham the money lender, concerning my letter of credit from Medici. He was delighted to give me as much gold as I needed. I took the opportunity to ask his views on setting up an Anglo-Italian bank in Southampton. He thought it was a very sound idea and actually offered me his eldest son young Abraham, as the manager to get me started, which I accepted on the spot. I knew no-one more experienced in money matters than the Abraham family. As I came out of the shop my old tutor, Brother Valerian, who had taught me illumination, came up to me and stared me in the face saying,

'Ned, is it you?'

I had to agree and once more we had a reunion conversation when he told me of how the scriptorium was faring. It seems nothing much had changed or progressed. As we were speaking, I saw young Sir Rollo FitzStephen walking towards us in the distance. He was scowling most fiercely and I stood close to Brother Valerian to protect him. As Rollo came up to me he stopped and shouted,

'You are no Italian prince! I know who you are. You are my wretched whipping boy Ned. Why are you dressed up like a popinjay?' He went on with a few more choice words. I was not afraid. I had already killed a vagabond and survived worse encounters. I forbore to argue but drew my sword and said quietly,

'Leave me Sir Rollo, You have already despoiled my wife, and it is only because of my son that I spare your life.'

In truth I was quite frightened. My position in society was high in Italy and I had become used to ordering other people around. Back in Winchester faced with my betters I reverted to my serf-like status. I was in fact, appalled at the insolent way I had spoken to one of the nobility. But I steeled myself, I thought why should I put up with this bully calling me names? I spoke again,

'You have no right to threaten me. You are a lecher and have fornicated with my wife. You should go down on your knees and beg my forgiveness.'

At this he became inflamed with fury, drew his own sword and flew at me using it like an axe and wielding it expertly like the trained swordsman he was. I stood no chance, my weapon is the longbow. He cut my sword arm and then my left shoulder and finally as I stumbled away he stabbed me in the thigh making me bleed most severely. Brother Valerian protested and made Rollo stop while he then attended to my wounds as best he could, but I was losing a deal of blood. Some kindly passers-by helped to put me on a baker's cart that was nearby and they wheeled me to the bishop's palace. There one of the servants helped Isabetta to bind my wounds. Isabetta was crying and sniffing and saying how England was such a God-forsaken country. The poor girl was sick with worry and fear.

I was in pain and fainting from the loss of blood and so could not help matters at all. I was sure that I was going to die.

Isabetta made an infusion of some herbs that Bishop William gave her and I fell asleep.

I awoke a day later and who was standing over my bed and wiping my forehead with a damp cloth but Emily my ex-wife. Apparently, she had arrived as soon as she had heard I was hurt, bringing little Justin with her. When Isabetta had found out who she was, a wary friendship developed. Slowly, sitting over me for two days together and talking animatedly, they came to understand and like one another.

Isabetta then told me that England seemed a much nicer place now that she had a friend. Each was so interested in the other's child.

Chapter 16

Amelia Gillies was now talking regularly to Tristan
Smallwood concerning the editing of the book. She
found that he was an experienced historian, (a first in
medieval history from Durham) and more competent
than she had expected. She was, as so many academics
are, quite surprised that someone outside the university
could actually read! In fact, his knowledge of Ned's
handwriting style and ancient English, was considerably
more thorough than hers. She then discovered that he
was a distant cousin of Baron Saye and Sele of
Broughton Castle. This was a place she had visited
several times from her childhood home in Banbury. Its
association with the Cromwell plotters appealed to her in
particular. Suddenly, Tristan seemed a handsome fellow
with great family connections. He was a bachelor and
intelligent and growing more attractive every time they
met. She didn't mention this either to Edward Clarke or
to Robert Simms. After a couple of months of their co-
operation on the journal it became evident that they were
drawn to one another romantically. Tristan invited
Amelia to visit Oxford with him to do some research in
the Bodlean library. They took a room in the Randolf
hotel and became enthusiastic lovers despite a certain age

difference.

§

When I finally came to, my jaw was still very painful. I was told that I had fallen heavily on it when Rollo stabbed me. I found that Isabetta had been chewing my meat for me and giving it to me in tiny portions to help me recover. I was able to take little Justin in my arms and enjoy the smell of him that I had missed. It seems that Sir Rollo had been somewhat ashamed of his attack and had allowed Emily to visit me as a kind of apology, for which I am most thankful. I have arranged with Abraham in Jewry Street to allow a small sum each month to Sir Rollo to be paid to the bailiff, to cover the expense and education of my son Justin as long as he looks after him. After a week I could walk with a stick and I sent for Simon to ask if he had found a suitable site for my bank. He had not finished searching but had three possible places so far. The one I liked was an abandoned tavern site above Bar. Simon had thought it would be too expensive to demolish completely before building but he had no notion of how much money I had. I discovered from asking around that it had been for sale without any interest shown for the past two years. I told the owner that I would buy it for the asking price but only if he cleared it first. After a short while, I could see that he was only too glad to agree.

Meanwhile, I was determined to find a cargo to take back to Genoa with me. Italians were so fond of English wool, that I knew exactly what I needed. Before leaving Italy, I had obtained a letter of recommendation from Peruzzi the foremost wool merchant in Firenze, certifying that I was a genuine trader. His company had already paid the Cistercian abbey at Bruern near Witney in Oxfordshire for twenty year's worth of wool in advance.

I hired a couple of four wheel wagons, each with two strong horses to draw them and with Simon and my two manservants began the 70 miles to Witney. The four of us were strong and looked quite dangerous with our swords. I had obtained a fine longbow and a sheaf of arrows by this time. We felt able to frighten off any thieves or vagabonds. My leg had healed as well as it might, but Brother Valerian said I might limp a bit for a few months.

I left Isabetta and the baby with Bishop William while we enjoyed a week crossing through the beautiful countryside of England. It was evident that since the plague there were nowadays far more sheep in the farmlands than either people or crops. We journeyed through New Burgh where a substantial market was the main attraction. Then on to Oxford where I had hoped to find great centres of learning. However, the city seemed to have lost its heart after the pestilence and much of it was uninhabited and sad to see.

It was easy to find a tavern or hostelry to stay each night and the three of us told many a tale as we journeyed. I had the letters of credit which would make certain of the purchase of wool, and my share would be paid to me by the Medici in Firenze on delivery.

Once we reached the abbey, the abbot came out to meet us. I had changed into my finest clothes and the impression was certainly working as he greeted us as if we were long lost pilgrims. Simon and I were entertained royally in the main dining hall and my two men given all the food and small beer that they could manage. The abbot said he had been expecting us all year and that the 100 sacks of wool were ready in the barn and all packed to go. We stayed for the evening service and another meal and were shown to clean but comfortable rooms. In the morning after early mass and a good breakfast, we helped the monks to load all the wool sacks onto our two waggons which were, as a result, very heavily laden. We set off at about ten of the clock and proceeded much more slowly than we had arrived. I decided to miss Oxford and we aimed directly for New Burgh. Each night one of the men slept on the sacks of wool as guard. They said that it was a pleasant duty, as it was more comfortable than some of the taverns we found on the way. It took ten days to reach Winchester. There we celebrated with Isabetta and the bishop before taking the cargo to Southampton and housing it all in a secure warehouse on the dockside ready for shipment with Captain Forester in the *Nostra Dame* which was due within the week.

My next concern was for the new bank I hoped I could establish in Southampton after the fashion of the Medici. I mentioned this to Bishop William who was immediately interested.

'My dear boy,' he said, 'I have been looking for an investment for the diocese, would it suit you to have the church as a partner?'

'Indeed it would,' I replied, 'I have been worried about the work being overseen when I am back in Italy.' And so it was arranged that the church would invest a third of the money for the bank in return for a third of the profits. The bishop would personally supervise the building and the start of the enterprise and young Abraham would be the first manager. I asked the bishop if he objected to a Jew being in charge of the banking. His reply was reassuring,

'Who better? Don't forget that Jesus was a Jew.'

It has now been upwards of a moon since my last entry, and although we have been exceedingly busy, nothing untoward has ocurred to give me unease. We are safely back in Firenze, having delivered the wool and been handsomely paid. I am now persuaded how rich men retain their money and make more and more. Until this year, I had not realised how easily money maketh money.

We are now going to visit my castle at Monte Ariggio at last only a few leagues from Firenze.
We set off in the carriage with Isabetta and Dominica inside with the baby. Simon and the ten other retainers and I rode horses. I had contracted eight more men as general guards and workmen in case there were many more repairs than expected. We had heard no word from Ralf who had been in charge of the castle since we left for England.
As we rode out of the Firenze walls Simon spotted a horseman riding towards us and shouted out that it was Ralf himself. When he came closer we could see that he was wounded and swaying about in the saddle. He stopped by the carriage and leaned out from the horse to support himself on the side of it. He spoke thickly as if his mouth was filled with spittle or blood.

'It's vagabonds, they've taken over the castle. Killed the other servants and now eating all our provisions.'
Ralf then slid to the ground and I could see that he was bleeding from a wound in his side and his arm. I wondered how he had managed to ride five or more leagues. Two men lifted him into the spare seat in the carriage and laid him down. Isabetta immediately took off his jerkin and bound the worst wound in his side. Dominica too helped with his arm and the application of balm and vinegar. I could see that Ralf was already

feeling eased in our company and he began to talk,

'As soon as I arrived two months agon, the farmers warned me of the gangs roaming locally, probably around ten men altogether. At first they were begging and then threatening. They stole any implements they could find and they were well-armed. We thought they could never attack the castle which had sound walls even though the furniture and kitchen garden were neglected. But last night three of them managed to climb the back wall and they roamed around inside until they found poor Maria the serving girl, raped her and killed Antonio my servant.'

He paused and asked for some water which we gave him.

'When I awoke I tried to attack them with my sword but there were too many and I only just managed to find my horse and escape in the dark. There is a secret trapdoor from the cellar...' Rollo then burst into tears as much from relief as fear and fell into a swoon.

I said that we should keep him with us, as Isabetta would take better care of him than any strangers, and continue to the castle. In the meantime I sent Simon back in to the city to recruit half a dozen more soldiers with crossbows and swords, offering extra pay.

We moved slowly towards Monte Ariggio tarrying so that Simon could catch up. We had to stop and make camp as daylight ended and he had still not arrived. During the night we heard the jangling of harnesses and dear Simon arrived with ten horse soldiers fully armed, so that we had twenty-one of us altogether. At first light we left Isabetta with Ralf in the camp well hidden from the road and guarded by two of the soldiers. I took the large bunch of the castle keys which Ralf had hung from his belt. The rest of us rode the next few leagues to within sight if the castle. It was my first view of my new

131

property and our future home. I had been told that it was built from the Alberesi limestone from the quarry at Bagno Vignoni. It sounded very special and I felt that I could not complain of my present lot. God had sent the pestilence all those years ago and without it I would never have come to Italy and been promoted by the pope so readily. The unfortunates who now roamed the countryside were the result of years of abandonment caused by God's will. But rape and murder must never go unpunished, nor should the occupation of the castle.

I took the opportunity to call on two of my farmers. I tried to reassure them that they would be safe now and how grateful I was for their loyalty and their rent. I think they were surprised to be addressed civilly by a foreigner. It seems the previous landlord had been very distant and uncaring. I was interested to find that one of the farms was actually a large vineyard and that the wine was greatly to my taste. I arranged for all the men to have enough wine to satisfy them and give them courage. Simon and I decided to wait for nightfall before attacking the castle. We would enter by the same secret doorway to the cellar from which Ralf escaped.

Chapter 17

Tristan Smallwood and Amelia spent two days exploring
Oxford and each other, looking at the sights and drinking
in the atmosphere of the city before arriving at the
Bodlean Library for their research. As graduates from
Durham and from Cambridge, the opportunity to soak
up the famous sights of the many Oxford colleges was
fulfilling their dreams.

It was not long before they had both discovered that there
were a number of contemporary books from the 13th
and 14th centuries written by travellers and pilgrims. The
book of Margery Kemp was of some interest, although
very spiritual compared with Ned Scrivener. Nevertheless,
it confirmed a great deal of the background information,
especially regarding the status and interests of pilgrims.
Margery was an indomitable but illiterate traveller, who
could not write about her adventures all over Europe
herself, but dictated her book to two priests. Another
useful reference was Julian of Norwich whose 'A
Revelation of Divine Love' provided numerous insights
into the attitudes to the church revealed by Ned.

Amelia had read a number of similar publications when
she studied for her doctorate, but had forgotten most of
them. In the end both she and Tristan thought that

further cross-referencing was of little use in the editing and translation of the journal.

'Do you think this diary is a complicated forgery?' Amelia asked Tristan.

'Not a chance, I've checked the parchment and the ink and all the internal evidence is irrefutable. Old Ned was a real scribe alright.'

Amelia now wanted to refine and re-write her own manuscript but was in no hurry to complete the work. She wondered whether she should talk it over with Professor Edward Clarke but Tristan was against this. He confided to her the plan of the Dean and Chapter to put the original up for auction with Sotheby's as soon as the translation was in the cathedral bookshop. Amelia was curious as to who might buy it and agreed that an American university or collector was probably the most likely.

§

As soon as night fell I lined up our small army and we filed on foot silently towards the castle and the secret entrance which Ralf had described to us. It was difficult to find in the dark and I would not allow any torches to be lit. Finally one of the sharp-eyed men whispered,

'Here it is your honour.' and I saw the tiny dark wooden door low down at the base of the wall.

'How did Ralf get his horse out through here?' I asked Simon.

'He did not, it was in the small stable nearby,' he laughed.

I led the way into the dark cellar where at last I lit a small torch. There was a set of straight stairs leading up to a door. I climbed up followed by Simon with drawn sword, and a soldier with his crossbow armed and ready. The door was locked and so I had to spend some time finding a key from the large ring that fitted. Eventually, I did so but opening the door made a loud noise which woke someone on the floor above who called out,

'Who's there?'

Silently, all nineteen of us moved into the hall which had a stone floor. I lifted the torch to try to see my new home. I was so unfamiliar with the place. I had never seen it in daylight. I suddenly became very angry at the unwanted intrusion of these wild men. Ahead of us there was a winding staircase which I supposed led up to the room where the men were sleeping. There did not seem to be a guard at this level. In pairs side by side we ran up as quickly as we could to the floor where we had heard the cry. As we reached the top several figures in states of undress rose with swords to try and stop us. Simon hacked at the first with his sword and cut the man's arm so badly that he had to drop his weapon. I held my torch high to see what was going on and my men rushed past me in a surprise attack on the still sleepy intruders. It was soon over with one of their number dead and several severely wounded from the enthusiasm of my followers. The leader, who was a huge giant of a man with a shaven head surrendered quickly and threw down his sword.

'I am called Serafino!' he called out, 'please forgive us for sheltering in your house. We are poor men, we meant no harm.'

Of course I was filled with fury and I strode up to this man and poked him in the chest with my sword.

'No harm? You have raped my servant and killed one of my retainers. You wounded my bailiff. You should all die for this.'

The giant fell to the floor on his knees,

'Please listen to me your honour,' he cried, 'I could not control these men, we are not a disciplined army. I gave strict orders not to harm any women or to kill servants. My men were drunk. I have punished them for what they did, but if I turn my back they will murder me.'

I confess I was astonished at this strange reaction and his confessions.

'Which one of you raped the girl and killed my servant? I asked looking round.

'It was Marco,' they all replied as one man, pointing to one of the bodies on the floor. He was dead.

'God has seen to this,' I said, I turned to my faithful Simon, 'Find a safe room and lock them all up until morning. Then I will decide what to do with them.'

We all slept on the same floor as the criminals had chosen and woke at daylight. I immediately began to explore the castle. It was not a large building, more like a tower some six stories high with small windows on four sides. Each floor consisted of only one main room and one or two small chambers. I could see how with some improvements, it could be a pleasant home.

I sent one of the men to bring Isabetta and Ralf back, I needed to ask Ralf many questions as he had been living here for a while.

With Simon and with Isabetta, I decided to interview each of the gang individually to try and discover the truth. I knew Simon was experienced and that Isabetta has an uncanny instinct with people. I let the vagabonds out of their locked room one by one. The first was looking sorry for himself, but that did not move me at all. We each asked him two or three questions and in particular, did the leader truly order them not to kill or to rape. He said that it was true but they did not care. We all agreed that he had no remorse, nor even pretended to. Each one of the rest was exactly the same, unrepentant and surly but agreed that Serafino had attempted to stop them more than once but they could not understand why. They may not have been murderers but they were certainly never going to impress the magistrate. Finally, we interviewed the big man who called himself Serafino. He emerged with his head hung low and looking remorseful.

'I am sorry for what has happened,' he muttered, 'I tried to keep some order but I was weak.'

'If you were so weak, why were you the leader?' I asked,'

'Because I am so big and also strong.' He showed his muscles, 'I also have better ideas than those simpletons, I made plans to save us from starvation which worked. At first they were satisfied with me.'
He paused and looked at the three of us in turn.

'Is there any way that I can make repentance to you? Please just say the word.'
Isabetta spoke first,

'I believe this man, what say you Simon?' Simon agreed and I was prepared to give the man a chance.

'Are you willing to work for me without pay but for your bread and board for one year' I asked.

'What work your honour?' said Serafino.

'Honest and heavy,' I replied.

'I would lief believe you signor and you will not be sorry, but please do not put me in charge of any other men.'
I replied without smiling,

'Your first task is to clean this whole castle from top

to bottom.'

I had myself known hunger and beatings and the evil effects of such a life on a person. Somehow, I think there is good in this Serafino and I was fain to take a chance. If he is true to his word, he may make a useful member of my family. Bread and board for a year guaranteed, would surely seem a good bargain for such as him. I sent the other men to the magistrates in Firenze under guard.

Now began a new domestic time in all our lives. With help of the men-at-arms and other servants, every chamber was cleared and cleaned and fresh straw laid where needed. I rode out and visited all ten of my holdings and attempted to make friends with every farmer. This was not always possible as farmers hate change. Many were worried that I was going to criticise or even turn them out of their houses. Once I had made it plain that neither of those things were likely as long as they co-operated and carried on with the work, they relaxed. Some were uneasy at having a foreigner as a landlord. (I found out that being a foreigner, meant that I came from Firenze!) Two of my farms were being run by elderly widows who had lost their menfolk in the pestilence.

I made Serafino grow his hair long, and with a new smock and sturdy boots, no-one in the area recognised the former leader of the vagabond gang. I offered his help to the two widows whenever they had any heavy work and they were delighted. I also noticed that Dominica our midwife had her eye on Fino, as he was now called by all.

Isabetta and I went often into Firenze in the carriage. She chose embroidery and hangings as well as much wooden furniture and tables. The men cleaned out the old privies and made some ditches to divert running water through them. Simon had persuaded his wife Lisa to join us as a sort of housekeeper and ladies' maid. This suited Isabetta as they were great friends and were to be found giggling together at all times of the day.

Ralf is now fully recovered, and as my marshall has charge of all the horses. He and some of the men have built a new large stable where he prefers to live in comfortable quarters with his wife and child.

Signor Poggio came to see me one day from the scriptorium in Firenze. He told me how he missed me and that they had much work that I could help with if I was willing. Of course I said yes, and then I showed him the upper room where I have made my own scriptorium. I had the men widen the narrow window to improve the light and build a lectern. I was already making some scrolls with illustrations. I had come to think that I would like an achievement of arms of my own and to perhaps make a flag. I thought at first of a drawing of William Tell, but he was a crossbowman and so I had outlined the shape of an English archer. Poggio expressed some interest but he said he needed my help, especially for the more complex tasks. He promised to send vellum and colours with the copies for orders on a regular basis if I was willing. I could work in my own home. Of course I agreed. Privately, I thought that there would be no other prince in Italy who would also be doing the work of a scribe!

§

When the edited and shortened version of the journal of Ned Scrivener finally appeared on sale in the Cathedral bookshop, it was something of a damp squib. It was a beautifully produced hard back; glossy and with a medieval-looking design of a scribe at his desk in full colour on the cover. Priced at £30 it was too expensive for an impulse buy and too cheap for the academic history market. Amelia did not mind as she had no contract for royalties, just the £250 fee for the work. It looked good on her CV as a published volume and she had met the man of her life, Tristan Smallwood.

Very few copies were sold, but then the Dean and the Bishop were unconcerned because they had at last firmly established their own copyright.

It now remained to get the leather bound original journal sold at auction. One of the canons with a lifetime experience of journalism, wrote a puff for the Church Times about the precious find in the cathedral roof. The Bishop prevailed upon an old friend of his from Oxford to review the cathedral shop edition favourably in the Telegraph colour supplement. The BBC website picked up the story and a few history bloggers followed that up. Sir Quentin FitzStephen from Sothebys, who had been fascinated by his namesake in the journal and claimed direct descendancy, wrote a quite scholarly article in the Sotheby's monthly newsletter which pleased the Dean and Chapter, because it began the long and difficult peregrination into the international world of auctioneering.

On the minus side Robert Simms, who had not been seeing Amelia for a month, had driven to Winchester from Reading to find out what had been going on. He knocked at the door of her flat in Oram's Arbour and was taken aback when Tristan Smallwood in his underwear answered at three in the afternoon. To say he was surprised would be an understatement, akin to describing World War Two as a skirmish. Not being made of stern stuff Robert turned and ran.

Professor and Diana Clarke had packed their bags for the flight to Florence, to take off as soon as the term ended. They would not leave until the last minute as the professor was still waiting to obtain a research grant to fund their trip. He had applied to the Arts and Humanities Research Council in Swindon and to the British Academy for a Mid-Career Fellowship. He was not prepared to approach more than two at a time, as he knew how they checked up with one another. So far he had not even had a reply or an acknowledgement from either.

Chapter 18

The copying work from Poggio is fascinating as I am now
receiving parchments from East Europe and Muscovy in
exchange for many Italian and English works. These all
need to be copied for the Firenze libraries and even for
the Vatican. I sometimes find myself working on a Coptic
scroll up to three times. Anything that interests me in
particular, I have Poggio's permission to copy for my own
collection. This is in lieu of any fee.

My vineyard is now becoming of great interest to me. I
have read all I can find about the proper care of vines
and together with the old viticoltore who runs the place,
we intend to improve the vino for putting into bottles and
to sell in the city. I am hoping that the Monte Ariggio
name will one day become synonymous with fine wine. I
mean to invite Cardinal Mosto to the castle when all is
ready, as I am sure he will recommend our vino in all the
right places.
This morning my marshall Ralf reported that he has
found two of my horses severely wounded, Ranuncolo
and Pratolina. They were both in the exercise yard
alongside the new stables. It is clearly no accident. The
poor creatures have been struck by weapons, most
probably crossbow bolts. One unfortunately died with a

stomach wound, the other is hanging on in such pain with a gash in the thigh that Ralf has already decided to kill it to be kind. They were two of my best horses. Of course they can easily be replaced, but they had a special place in our hearts, especially with Ralf's little daughter Ellen.

I have decided to begin hunting. All my life I have seen the gentry riding to hunt and wondered how it felt to put ones wits against a wily prey. In the forest around Winchester there were many deer and boar, but of course as a humble serf, I only heard tell of the hunt. Now I had land, men and horses and it was time I experienced la caccia as we say in Italy. Both Simon and I wished to practice the longbow on horseback. We could see that it would not be easy. Most hunters here use spears or crossbow. We also needed dogs and so I acquired a small pack of alaunt, which were among the local favourites for hunting the hart.

The first morning we set off was something of a disaster. The dogs outran us and disappeared yelping and delighted to be free. We followed as quickly as we could and eventually in the thickest part of the forest we saw a huge male hart about two hundred paces away. The dogs were surrounding the beast and barking. Simon and I both sent arrows but they hit the branches of trees as it was too difficult to aim well even from a still horse. Laughing, we descended on foot and crept further ahead towards where we had seen the hart. Of course, it was long gone before we got much nearer. It then came on to rain heavily and we re-mounted and rode home wet, bedraggled and with our men in a poor mood.

I hope to write further about a more successful, hunt one day.

I have replaced the two lost horses and Ralf has named them Quill and Vellum thinking to please me. As vellum is cow-skin I doubt the horse would approve, but they are easy to remember, and he has already painted the names on their stalls.

***

It is said that a happy man loses ambition. In my case I have neglected my journal of late and it must be at least three moons since I wrote last. I sit down to write this day because Fino my giant servant has proved faithful, and has asked if he can marry the nurse Dominica. They are both happy with each other and so I have agreed. It will soon be a year that Fino has served me, but I think he will want to become a permanent member of the family. A week agon he came into the castle yard pulling a helpless looking fellow by the hair and holding a broken crossbow in his other hand. I saw him throw his captive down on the ground below the steps to the door and to my surprise I recognised Matthias the scribe from Master Poggio's scriptorium in Firenze. Fino shouted,

'Here is the villain that killed our horses your honour! I found him about to shoot another.'
I hastened down to the doorway and told Fino to bring Matthias inside. He was half dead from his torture. I called for water and one of the maids came with a jug. I thought of Our Lord and what he might do, so gave him a drink and had Dominica to bind up his wounds. I thanked Fino but made it clear that I knew the miscreant and would deal with him in my own way.
When the fellow came out of his swoon he looked weak, starved and sheepish. I knew him to be of poor temper and asked him what he was doing shooting horses. It was

a crime that could result in him being branded or sent to the galleys for life.

At this he broke down and was inconsolable. I gathered that he had lost his position as a senior scribe, for drunkeness and for missing many days of work. He had become fixed of the notion that I was to blame for all his misfortunes. The poor fellow was out of his mind. I told Isabetta and Dominica both to feed him and make him rest.

This morning I received a letter from Bishop William to inform me that the bank in Southampton was built and ready to open. I was needed to be there and to help with many decisions. This means I will have to travel to England once again, but this time I wanted to take Simon only with me and leave my family under the protection of Ralf and the servants. Simon asked if he could bring his wife Lisa with him and I agreed readily.

I do not have the heart to give Matthias up to the magistrates so I may have to keep him as a prisoner. It is a difficult complication. I will ask Ralf what he thinks as it was the horses under his care that were killed.

Ralf has come up with a solution. He suggests that I write a legal paper for Matthias to sign promising to stay within the castle until I return. He could possibly do some of the less important copying in my scriptorium. It might help to heal his mind. I may then give him the option to work for me (as happened with Fino) or take his chance with the law. If he absconds, he may as well be banished, for that is how we should treat him. Fino is willing to be his jailer as he understands his position better than anyone.

§

Canon Felicity James had tired of waiting to be asked to put together a miracle play for the cathedral. She had made the suggestion to the Dean in good faith and he seemed to be encouraging at the time. In fact he had immediately forgotten the request. Her last post was as head of drama and religious studies in a Middlesex comprehensive school. There she was queen of the theatre performances. Everyone was keen and she was popular as a result. She had applied to Winchester for this minor canonship, as it was a step up in her career and she was curious to find out more about the traditional side of church life. What she did not know was that for weeks before, the Bishop had been asking the Dean why there were so few women working in the cathedral, apart from the 400 or so lay volunteers! The Dean had immediately picked out Felicity's application when it arrived and agreed to it before you could say ecumenical.

When she started work and quickly became known as the Cockney Canon, the Dean regretted his haste and had tried to pretend that she did not exist. This was not only deeply snobbish, but infair and unkind because Felicity had always succeeded in the past and been well-loved, even though a bit scatty.

Her partner and loved one, Gillian Parsons, who had soon found a post in Winchester as a sort of roving curate, was irate about the miracle play.

'They haven't even given you a copy of this journal thing. So how are you supposed to get on with it anyway?'

'I know, I fink I'd better drop in and see Brian about it today.'

Just before midday Felicity arrived at the cathedral office, went in, and knocking briefly at the Dean's door she entered. There was the Dean at his computer screen totally absorbed in a search of some kind. He had not heard Felicity, so curiosity pulled her across the soundless carpet to peer at the screen. The page was one devoted to sales records for the major auction houses, Bonham's, Christie's and others. She spotted a sub-heading, "Medieval manuscripts" and a table of dates sold and prices in New York, Paris, Berlin and Moscow. The Dean had a small notebook and was copying some of the details down in a tight italic hand. Felicity noticed numbers, that looked like 1.6 million, 2.5 million before she was heard and the Dean looked up.

'Oh hello Brian! I just fought I'd drop in and see how fings was getting on.'

'Getting on? What things?'

'We talked abaht a miracle play; I was hopin' you'd give me some clues as to want you wanted. I fought the deanery garden...'

'Miracle play? Whatever gave you that idea woman? You can see how busy I am. Please get out of my office.'

'Ooh! Pardon me I'm sure,' muttered Felicity very put out by her reception. She went straight back home to tell Gillian all about it and to have a little cry.

Chapter 19

The voyage to Southampton was uneventful. I travelled
in a ship that I had never seen before, which had an
Italian captain. He was a pleasant fellow called Giuseppe
and we had many conversations about religion and
politics in the evenings over a glass or two of wine. I
formed the impression that he was a better seaman than
my old friend Captain Forester as we were not blown off
course and never went backwards. Giuseppe was
impressed that I had saved the Pope's life. He then
regaled me with tales of pirates and how he had once
been captured and ransomed by them on this very route.
When I confessed that I had started life as a humble serf,
he showed astonishment, as he had also begun as a lowly
ship's boy and servant to all. By diligent application to
learning navigation and mathematics he had, over thirty
years worked himself up to a captain.

Once ashore in Southampton with Simon and Lisa we
repaired to the site of the Bank. It looked small but a
well-built edifice with a painted sign hanging outside
saying "Anglo-Italian Bank in association with ye
Church". It had not opened properly yet and I brought
the letters of credit from my bankers the Medici brothers
in Firenze. Abraham the elder was there with his son to

stock the cellar with nobles upon receiving the letters. I had also brought 100 florins in cash with me to add to the bank's hoard. The interior was bare but business-like with two full sets of scales and weights. The cellar was secure containing four locked strong boxes, yet to be filled. Bishop William planned to increase the capacity of the bank as quickly as possible.

I stayed for two days and went through all the business matters required. I sent Simon and Lisa to the Bishop's palace to await me, as once more we had been invited to stay as long as we liked.

When I arrived in Winchester, All my old friends were there to recognise me. It was quite a different scene from the first time I returned. Justin the bailiff and Giles the marshall were outside the palace gate. Brother Robert my archery tutor, Aleric and Athelstan the bookbinder who had made this journal, as well as my illumination tutor Brother Valerian were also present. All were pleased to see me and glad of my good fortune. Tears came to my eyes as I greeted them all. Justin had organised a feast for all of us at the God Begot Inn. So with Simon and Lisa and a promise to visit later from Bishop William, we sat around four large tables which had been pushed together and caroused late into the night.

By noon the next day I was recovering in the palace parlour with a small beer and some shellfish, when Simon sat beside me and asked if we might speak together.

He told me that Lisa had, to his surprise, discovered that she loved England and had begged him to see if they could stay. He told me that he also was hoping to better himself and to find some suitable work in the area of Winchester. He still had some family not too far away. My first reaction was disappointment. How could I do without my trusted bailiff? But then I began to use my good sense. I would always need a loyal friend in England now that I had business here. I was also thinking of expanding into the wool trade and of buying a ship of my own.

'Simon,' I said, 'would you like to be my agent here and to oversee everything for me?'

'I don't know what to say Ned,' he took both my hands and knelt down in gratitude.

'Get up man, I owe you more than I can say. Do you accept?'

He did of course, and now the more I think of it the better the idea becomes.

***

I am back home in domestic bliss once again. I had travelled back by sea without mishap. Isabetta was so welcoming that I never had any occasion to regret marrying a humble Italian maid, for she was as clever a princess as could be found. I had parted with Simon and Lisa with some tears on their part. I have rented a handsome house for them in the city of Winchester and I have no doubt Simon will become a distinguished burgher in time.

Life must go on in Monte Ariggio and I found that in my absence Matthias had carried out some very creditable copy work in my scriptorium and seemed to have settled in well. I still do not trust him completely, although Fino seems to have convinced him of my good intentions if he wished to respond.

This morning, Matthias came to me as I was walking the grounds of the castle. I love to watch the changing of the leaves on the trees and to check the vegetable garden. I have planted a large variety of medicinal herbs too. He walked alongside me for ten minutes or so and I suspected he was plucking up the nerve to ask for his release. To my surprise he suddenly fell on his knees and took my right hand in his.

'Prince, I am sorry for all I have done, not just the horses, but how I disliked you for no real reason when you first came to Firenze. I admit it was jealousy. You were a foreigner and more skilled than I.'
He began to sob uncontrollably, holding onto my hand and begging for forgiveness. He went on,

'Your kindness has shown me the ways in which I have wronged you...' etcetera etcetera. It was uncomfortable to listen to, although I have to admit that what he said was true. It seems that he had been given several lectures about his good fortune from Fino while I was away, which clearly had their effect. Consequently, he had made a great effort with the copying, which was gratifying as he was still a good scribe.
I spoke to him like a father,

'Please get up Matthias, I am an ordinary man like you. When we first met you knew nothing of me, but I tell you I had a more humble beginning than you. I was born a serf.' I then told him briefly about my life and how I owed much to good men who had trusted and helped me in many things. My aim now was to repay their example by doing likewise. Suddenly I had an idea,

'Simon has stayed in England, I need another trusted right-hand man. I cannot make you my bailiff, but I could use you as a secretary because you can read and write. If you take the position and prove yourself trustworthy for a year or two, I will see what else I may do. I will pay you a good wage but you must foreswear the drinking..'

Matthias seemed overcome. He was not used to receiving good for ill and was lost for words for a minute, then,

'I will be your secretary for as long as you wish. You have given me hope after I was abandoned by Master Poggio. Thank you, you truly are a prince among men.' Then he said a few other flattering things which I shall not repeat here.

And so it has become that I have a secretary now, which will absolve me of many duties and help with the copy work.

I receive a report by letter once a month from Simon. He is still practicing the longbow every week. He visits the Bank in Southampton at least twice a month and has looked at three ships with a view to us buying one soon. So far, he has not been impressed with their soundness. Isabetta is with child again and we are hoping for a girl.

§

The airport was as crowded as usual and Diana Clarke was already flustered by the train journey from Winchester to Heathrow. Now she and Edward had to join the long queues for the baggage check-in for Rome's Leonardo da Vinci airport. Edward seemed completely happy and at ease. She knew that this next stage of his quest for information on Ned Scrivener excited him more than any of his previous projects. However, she was already fed up with the whole thing, and only the prospect of some sun and Italian food was keeping her spirits from sinking to floor level.

Finally, they were in the Airbus and the long taxi to take-off was again making her feel anxious and yet ashamed to be so.

The flight was like almost all commercial flights these days, boring and without any real feeling of movement. Diana believed that since air travel had become mundane, you could arrive at some airport with no idea of whether it was north or south, or west of your home country Being above cloud most of the time snatched away what interest there may have once been in taking a journey, even a pilgrimage. As they descended down the West coast of Italy, the sudden sight of the Carrera marble quarries came as a pleasant surprise and a reality check for both the Clarkes and helped to convince Diana that they were truly on their way to Italy. Edward had chosen Rome to begin their quest, rather than Florence as he thought there would be more family records in the institutions there.

The Hotel de Monte on the Via Panisperna in central Rome was Edward's choice for their stay. He had spent about an hour on the internet and was finally impressed by Trip Advisor which gave it five stars, even though it was small and inexpensive.

The professor had already found that searching for medieval family records in Italy was not easy. There is a lot of information online but nearly all date from the records made by Napoleon's civil servants 1806-1815. These are referred to as the vital records. Before that most records, if kept at all, were the work of the churches in the various city states. They had travelled to Italy to look at what rare historic traces could be found by personal search.

On the first morning Professor Edward Clarke set out with head held high to seek out the most likely places to find any medieval family records. Diana went shopping.

§

It is time to invite Cardinal Mosto to my castle and to play host publicly to a senior Vatican official. The cardinal has been instrumental in my fortune and advancement and I feel that I can never repay him. I am sure he is curious however, as to how I have been faring. I have written to him and his reply came swiftly and with great friendship this afternoon. He asked if he might bring a young friend and protégé called Galileo Rigotto. This I found amusing of course and in my new position as a sophisticated member of the nobility, accepted the description of his catamite without question. He promised to be with us within a sennight.

I have asked Matthias to order extra food and have as much wine sent up from our vineyard as would be necessary. I worked out from memory that the Cardinal seldom travelled anywhere without six armed guards and two scribes. There would be at least eight ridden horses and four more for his carriage. So fodder and accommodation would have to be arranged. This all would be a useful test for Matthias in his new post, but I instructed Ralf alone to make all the arrangements for the horses.

Isabetta is sick in the mornings and having slightly more difficulty with this present confinement than before. I have summoned an apothecary to stay with us until her time. Dominica is in constant attendance. I shall arrange for Isabetta and her helpers to remain in her quarters during the cardinal's visit as I know from experience that Mosto is badly affected by anything to do with women and their lives, especially childbirth.

I am besotted with our little Piero, according to Dominica, but I do love him so. I played with my first son Justin and enjoyed his company too, but Piero is the apple of my eye, perhaps because I am able to give him anything he needs. This reminds me however, that I must send to Simon to arrange with my bank for a larger monetary supply for Justin and his education.

Mosto arrived yesterday. We were so happy to see one another. He told me that although I was a great loss to my profession as a translator and scribe, I was doing well as a landowner, banker, and winemaker! He was surprised to hear of my business interests in England, and pleased to meet Fino and Matthias as examples of forgiveness and reformation. He insisted on blessing both men which impressed them mightily. Matthias was in tears once more as he knelt before the cardinal.

We went hunting today with Ralf in charge. Galileo Rigotto declined the invitation to hunt and said he would take a walk at the edge of the forest and pick some wildflowers. This time it was more successful as the cardinal bagged a large rabbit and Ralf himself a small deer. Mosto gave the rabbit to the dogs and we took the deer home for Fino to skin and hang. Galileo became lost in the forest and it took Fino two hours to find him. He declined any supper and went straight to bed on his return. We all consumed much wine in the evening and I am only just able to stay awake enough to write this journal.

This morning Mosto offered to baptise little Piero. Isabetta was overcome with emotion to have our son christened by a Vatican cardinal. Of course we agreed and I had Matthias hastily arrange a small party for our friends that afternoon. I had some contacts in Firenze such as the Medicis and my wool trader Peruzzi. All my farmers who could be spared, attended and it became a memorable occasion. When the cardinal left to return to

Rome, a large crowd of family and retainers gathered to wave him off he had proved a most popular visitor.

Chapter 20

The Archivio Segreto Vaticano is 322 yards approximately North-East of St Peter's Basilica in the Vatican. Professor Clarke had obtained prior permission to visit the archive, with all the conditions met. It was open to scholars every day from 0830 to 1300 and Edward meant to get there as it opened. He had his reader's card in hand and was not carrying his laptop or anything such as a camera or drink. He was admitted by the functionary and taken to the 14 th century stack and left in silence. He began by trying all the names he could remember from the journal. Ned Scrivener, Cardinal Mosto, Boniface IX with no useful results except for Poggio Bracciolini a well-known scribe in his day. His search for Prince de Monte Ariggio was not possible as all titles were abolished in 1946 when the Italian republic was formed. Records from the middle ages were not destroyed but they hardly existed outside their local areas He settled down to his second favourite activity, research in a huge quiet library.

Diana took a taxi to the Spanish Steps which was also the gateway to most of the upmarket fashion boutiques. The

Via Condotti boasts brands such as Gucci, Louis Vuitton, Armani and so on. She did not expect to buy anything but to drink in the atmosphere of wandering about feeling like a millionaire. She had Edward's credit card just in case though. The crowds were huge but non-threatening, good humoured and multi-national. The 1950s pastime of Italian men pinching the women's bottoms was practically unknown these days. So unmolested, Diana strode in the sunshine and enjoyed the adventure, so unlike walking down Winchester high street. It crossed her mind that the experience was probably very similar for this Ned person when he first came to Rome. She wondered briefly how Edward was getting on in the Vatican and whether she should meet him for lunch. She decided it would be much more fun to lunch alone. She spotted a tiny coffee bar, went in and ordered a cappuccino. The derision on the barman's face spoke volumes but he prepared it, and handed the cup over with a small but expressive shrug.

Sitting at the metallic circular table outside, she sipped her drink and noticed a handsome Italian, about her own age, watching her with admiration. This made up for the barista sneer and she smiled, this visit was beginning to improve.

§

I should be more disciplined as it is almost a twelve-month since I wrote anything in this book. Much has happened since Cardinal Mosto's visit to my home. Isabetta has had another son. She is amazingly blest with her births and we have named him Roberto after my old tutor in Winchester. He is a healthy stocky little fellow and already a source of fascination for his elder brother

Piero.

I have not travelled back to England as I find Italy feels so much more like my home now. According to Simon's regular letters, the bank in Southampton goes from strength to strength. I have letters from Bishop William too saying that the trade in wool has increased the profitability of the bank and it is now time to invest in a ship. I agree but I believe I should purchase a vessel in Genoa or Civitavecchia. Then I can inspect it for myself. I want a ship that is well-founded, roomy and with comfortable quarters for passengers and crew.

I have had such a shock this week, that I can hardly hold my pen to write. I have received two letters in the same delivery from Abraham the bank manager in Southampton and Bishop William. I will quote Abraham.

'My dear Prince, I have bad news, Simon, your agent has disappeared. He came to the bank on a regular visit last week and asked to draw out some money for your son's education as we have arranged long ago. I was busy in the back room with another customer and gave Simon the keys to the cellar and strong boxes as usual. This is so normal a procedure that I thought nothing of it. I am so sorry, but to continue. An hour or so later, I discovered that the cellar was still open and one of the coffers had gone. It contained at least half of the bank's fortune, about 500 pounds. I realised that Simon had brought four or five strong men with him and had chosen his time cleverly. He and his wife Lisa have gone. They must have planned this robbery for a long time.'

The bishop has more to say after describing the robbery much as Abraham had,

'My dear Ned, I am sorry to tell you that Simon,

whom I trusted as you did, has vanished with £500 of the bank's money. I have reports that he was seen going north probably towards London, also that he had developed a habit of gambling with dice and incurred many debts.'

I am struck down with grief. Simon was such an old and trusted friend that my faith in human nature has been badly affected. Who will be next to let me down? Serafino? Matthias? Ralf? I cannot bear to think of it. The money is nothing. That can be replaced. The trust that I had in my friends has gone. I would as lief believe that Bishop William would rob me.

I have taken to my bed and will write in this journal again when I have recovered my confidence.

§

The professor and Diana met later that day back in the Hotel de Monte and compared notes. Diana was the first to ask how Edward got on.

'In short, hopeless, but it was enjoyable getting back to some true research. I learned a lot about how to proceed I think, how about you?'

'Well, I had a lovely long look round the posh shops and and an excellent lunch.'

Her three hour assignation with the handsome Italian in his hotel room, remained a wonderful memory of shopping in Rome. She had thought about Dr Amelia Gillies for the three minutes it had taken her to undress and the rest of the time had been unspoken bliss. If he had known any English, he certainly did not reveal it; and Diana knew little or no Italian.

Edward pursued his point.

'If I'm to get anywhere it's obvious that Rome is not the place. Records are simply not centralised. We're going to have to go to Florence and to find the Castello Monte Ariggio.'

'But we've only just got here Ed, surely we can stay a day or two for some shopping? I didn't buy anything today, just window shopped.'

'You can stay darling, the room's booked for a week.'

'Perhaps I will,' answered Diana. She had the stranger's hotel number.

They retired for the night, and Edward booked a train to Florence the next morning.

'I'll phone you to say where I am love. Are you sure you'll be OK? You really should look in on the Vatican archive. It's terrific, you can take my reader's card.'

'Thanks, I might do that,' said Diana.

Edward found Florence a lot more to his taste. The pace and the crowds were slightly less frenetic than Rome. His hotel was comfortable but small, the hotel Duomo Firenze.
The staff at the Archivio de Stato Firenze were delighted to welcome him, especially as Edward had spent a lot of time already studying their website and was familiar with the place in general. However, this time he was after the specialist knowledge of the curator and others. He began with a list of the people mentioned in Ned's journal. They had no local records of Cardinal Mosto's visit, but after two or three hours of scanning through marriage records, there it was, the mention of a Prince Ariggio de Monte Ariggio married to Isabetta Bonavista June 5 th

1387.

To say that this was exciting was an understatement. Edward showed his printout of Ned's journal to the chief curator who was astonished and begged a copy from him. Disregarding all notions of copyright, Edward thought that the Archive had a right to a copy and allowed them to make one while he stood there. To celebrate, the chief curator suggested they go to his favourite restaurant for lunch.

By the time they had finished their meal, Edward did not feel like more research and so he returned to the hotel and lay down for a couple of hours trying to calm his sense of excitement and achievement. At last he had linked the journal to an actual person. The next unenviable task was to find out what happened to Ned and why this leather bound volume had been hidden in the Winchester cathedral roof? And more to the point are there any surviving descendents?

Chapter 21

After three moons I feel able to resume writing about my life. I have good friends and a wonderful wife and it a sin to fall into despair. I believe I am a natural optimist. Life at Castello Monte Ariggio has proceeded with little incident. Both Fino and Matthias have been at pains to justify my acceptance of them and were very angry when they heard about Simon.

The new baby Roberto is a constant delight and is being fussed over by Lucia his grandmother, Dominica, and curiously by the giant Serafino who takes him for walks in his arms when no-one else can get him to sleep. Just five minutes with Fino and he is completely out of this world. Three months income from my apartments in Rome has been enough to replace the lost money in the bank. However, we have all agreed a new security arrangement where no-one enters the cellar alone and two keys are now needed for both the cellar door and every coffer inside.

I shall be travelling to both Genoa and Civitavecchia soon to either purchase a ship or have one built. To own a ship will be to offset only four or five payments for the charter of other vessels. Also, I can lease my own ship to other traders and make a profit.

I have bought a beautiful ship in Genoa. She is only two
years old and belonged to a friend of Giovani di Bicci
de'Medici my banker in Firenze. It was assembled in
Genoa by the finest craftsmen. One of the first trading
vessels to be built since the port was sacked by the
Venetians. They seem to be a small state which having
become over rich from trading, now has ideas well above
its station and will attack anyone that they disagree with.
This purchase however, proves that it is not what you
know, but who you know. I was able to obtain the full
history of the vessel which was that a wool trader had lost
so much money on a bad cargo that he has had to sell his
ship, called the   *Vivande*. Giovani heard of this and
immediately wrote to me with the information. Now I am
going to hire a new captain Giuseppe Esposito whom I
met on my last trip to England. He seems delighted to
accept. I know he is a good, experienced and safe
captain.
I look forward to journeying back to England to inspect
my bank and perhaps to find Simon and hold him to
account.

My vines are doing well this year and the vinificatore has
told me that he expects the wine to be the best ever this
time. He has put a lot of effort into studying as well as
caring for the plants. I hope to make my wines of Monte
Ariggio to be highly sought after. It is better to have a
small crop of excellent vintage than a large yield of
indifferent wine.
Matthias is finally in my employment. I have decided to
trust him after discussing the Simon affair with him. He,
of course, ever since the archery contest all those years
ago, never liked Simon and has railed bitterly against his

lack of loyalty. He has sworn that he originally misjudged me, not knowing of my lowly birth. He has had every opportunity to leave my house and to disappear. I have set one or two traps for him by trusting him with large sums of money. He has behaved well and shown his faith and integrity. He and Fino have become good friends and I think that is the first real soulmate he has ever had. I am disposed to take Fino with me to England for my protection and for his education, while leaving my family and property under the charge of Matthias and Ralf equally. Giovani will countersign any money transactions that Matthias may have to make. I have made it clear however that I trust him. I cannot live with continual suspicion of those around me, but the actions of Simon have made me much more wary. Isabetta too is a wonderful check on what is going on. She has more wit in her little finger than anyone else I that know has in their head. Now that Simon's betrayal has warned us, she will not let anything go unnoticed while I am away.

§

Edward Clarke rose the following morning feeling as excited as he was the day before. Knowing that a genuine Prince Ariggio existed made his whole interest in the journal so far to be worth the effort. It seemed that the Archivio in Florence had helped him all they could and he would have to think of other sources to look into. The first thing to do would be to find Ned's castle which should be nearby. He had searched on the internet and could only find an hotel with that name, just a few miles from Florence. He hired a car for the day and drove out to the place. As he approached, he could see a building that looked much as Ned had described his home. When he arrived he found the hotel Monte Ariggio, a four star family establishment with several accompanying facilities, golf, riding, archery, and a white truffle hunt in the season October and November. Edward entered and asked to see the manager. A woman of about forty, very smart and sophisticated appeared and introduced herself as Signora Voltolini and asked him in perfect English what she could do for him. When he told her that he was researching the family who once owned the hotel when it was a castle, she became interested and asked him to take a seat while she arranged coffee for them.

'We have a leaflet with the story of the place, but it is quite sketchy about the middle ages. The history of the hotel as we know it, begins after world war two.'

'Who owns the hotel now?' asked Edward.

'It is an international company which has shipping and banking and many other interests. I believe it operates from New York. It is called Orbis.'

'Do you know the name of the family that owned it before it became a hotel?'

'No I don't, but I understand that there are no previous owners. It became an hotel without changing hands. We have, I believe, an unbroken history of ownership from time immemorial. But what makes you so interested in this establishment?'

Edward explained about the journal and that Ned was Prince Ariggio de Monte Ariggio and that the castle had been given to him by the Pope.

'This is all news to me of course. I am only an employee of the company, but someone high up in Orbis may know a little more, but I have no idea who to ask.'

Edward thanked Signora Voltolini and asked if he might take stroll around the grounds.

'Of course you are welcome, why not play a round of golf or something, on the house of course.

Edward laughed,

'I am no sportsman, I am afraid.'

'I understand, to many Englishmen golf is a good walk spoilt, yes?'

Edward wandered outside and round to the extensive lawns at the back. He saw a noticeboard obviously advertising archery. What was significant, judging by the pictures on the advert, they were offering the English longbow.

When he returned from his walk Diana was waiting for him in the bar, drink in hand.

'I guessed you would be here,' she said.

Edward kissed her and told her about the marriage record he had found. She was impressed, and said,

'Have you tried Ned's wine?'

'What do you mean?'

'I am drinking a very fine Tuscan red,' and she shewed him the bottle and her glass. It was labelled, Vino Prince Monte Ariggio.

'It could be from Ned's original vineyard, I must ask Signora Voltolini,' said Edward.

§

After three weeks on the *Vivandi* both Fino and I were longing to reach land. I was not ill but Fino suffered greatly from the *mal de mare*. For such a big strong man he had been like a child on board, quite unable to help himself or others. I felt so sorry that I had made him come with me.

I had spent much time talking philosophy with Giuseppe and exploring the ship from stem to stern. I became anxious for the first time when I saw water in the bilges, until Giuseppe laughed and said that it was important to keep the planks slightly wet so that they swelled and did not shrink. I can see that as a ship owner, I have much to learn.

I had not written to warn the bank that I was arriving this time. I thought to make an unexpected inspection of the security measures and the alertness of the workers. So when Fino and I arrived at the front door, we walked in and asked to see the person in charge. Fino looked around in wonder as he had never seen a bank before. The clerk stood up and stared at Serafino with suspicion as he was so tall and fairly rough-looking. He rang a handbell which was on the table before him. Young Abraham came running immediately. As soon as he saw me he laughed aloud and told the clerk not to worry as here was the owner of the bank all the way from Italy. Abraham and I exchanged news. He told me that he was now running the day to day business and his father was mainly back in Jewry street in Winchester lending and changing smaller amounts of money. There had been no word from Simon and everyone thought that he had fled to the north of England, to the wilder parts where there was little or no law. In the meantime I sent Fino off to explore Southampton and to return in an hour. I considered that it would be a good start to his education. I had taught him a small amount of English to help.

Abraham told me that several wool traders from the south of England whose ships sailed from Southampton, had put their trust in our bank and been very pleased with the ease which they could draw money in Italy. Two of them had placed all their recent profits with us for safe-keeping. The Simon incident had been kept quiet from the general public and so confidence in the bank had not been affected.

Fino returned from his walk around the port. No-one had threatened him and he had enjoyed the marvels of all the ships and the warehouses. He brought with him a huge salmon that he had bought cheaply from a stall. Such a fish is rare and expensive in Italy. We closed the bank and took Abraham to a nearby eating house where it was cooked for the three of us for our midday meal. I was pleased that Fino had shown such initiative.

Chapter 22

The cathedral archivist Tristan Smallwood had decided
to research the Winchester city records as well as the
cathedral archives, to see if there were any mentions of
the other people in Ned's journal. He thought it likely
that there would be a record of the FitzStephens as they
were local gentry from Twyford. The Sotheby's man,
Quentin FitzStephens, was convinced that he must be a
descendant of Lord Rollo and Ned's ex-wife Emily. The
only record Tristan could find was a very dilapidated set
of scrolls from the 14 th C apparently referring to births
and deaths in the parish of Twyford. There was an entry
of the death of Rollo FitzStephens on November 8th
1398 with a note that he was childless and his will left
everything to the church.

Amelia Gillies persuaded him to abandon any further
research. She was bored with the whole thing and wanted
to get on with her teaching. She had become
domesticated since moving in with the archivist. She had
even taken up cooking. They planned to go to Paris for

Christmas, and Tristan, who had fallen for her completely, was now as keen as she was to study the cuisine. Ned's journal was soon forgotten by the couple but not by the Dean Brian Woodward. He was making all kinds of arrangements for the sale through Sotheby's. He had contacts all over Europe and the United States putting short illustrated articles about the journal's discovery in different papers and magazines. It was his experience that if you wanted to sell something, you had to put it before the public as often as possible. If he had not been a priest he would have made a successful businessman.

§

Fino and I arrived quietly in Winchester and drove up to the Bishop's palace where I knew we would always be welcome. The bishop was not in residence, but his servants treated us like family and room was made for us to stay for as long as we liked. Bishop William was in London on church business and for an interview with the king.

After some refreshment, I left Fino to wander around the town and I went in search of my eldest son Justin. Borrowing one of the bishop's horses I rode out to the FitzStephen's place and the first person I saw was Giles the marshall in the stables and there was my little six year-old Justin helping with the horses exactly as I used to. It looked as if Giles and my son were repeating our old relationship and this time Justin was indeed his real grandson. Justin did not recognise me but nevertheless I picked him up and embraced him with loving words and kisses. He begged to be put down and ran to the marshall which was like a stiletto in my heart, although I understood the reason. When I had recovered myself I asked if my old tutor, brother Patrick was about. Giles told me that he had a small room at the back of the house and had become almost a hermit of late. I asked directions and made my way across to seek him.

When I found him reading quietly, he jumped up and was so pleased to see me in such contrast to Justin, that I confess a tear came to my eye.

'Ned my dear boy, I had heard of your good fortune but never expected to see you again!'

I answered him in like manner and we chatted about old times and how both Lord Rollo and myself had changed and become reconciled. I asked if he would be Justin's tutor now that he was approaching his seventh year.

'Let him play for a few more months and then I would be pleased to teach him his letters and some French and Latin,' said my wise master. I then told him how as a result of his particular teaching, I now spoke Italian like a native and could read and write some Arabic. I assured him that I would pay him a good fee, but he waved his hand and said that he lacked nothing and would be satisfied if Justin learned as well as his father. I resolved, however to lodge enough silver for

Justin's keep and education with Lord Rollo now that he had all but adopted my son. It was indeed an unusual situation for a lord to have married a simple maid, ex-wife of a serf, and to receive money for the son of the serf now turned a prince. I bade goodbye to Brother Patrick and looked for Lord Rollo to make the arrangement for a money transfer, but it appeared that he was out hunting. I found Emily in the garden putting horse manure on some roses. She was a country girl still and will never be a grand lady. We embraced modestly and she told me that Rollo was a kind and a good, if somewhat wayward, stepfather to Justin. She admitted that some more money would be welcome as the FitzStephen fortune was diminished considerably as the farms could not support the people in addition to Rollo's hunting and his horses. She suggested that I send the money to Giles and not to her husband who might be tempted to spend it on his own pursuits. I was surprised that Emily had become so canny, but as Giles was Justin's grandfather I thought it a wise idea and decided to take her advice.

On my return to the Bishop's palace, there was no sign of Fino, so I wandered into town to see where he might be and to soak myself in nostalgia for my old life. I spoke to Brother Robert and invited him to visit me in Florence one day. He would love to see the scriptorium where I first worked for Master Poggio. He said he would consider it. I told him he could have free travel at any time in my ship *Vivandi*. I found Fino eventually in Jewry street, working with old Abraham in his money lending house. It appears that Abraham sometimes has to take silver to traders in the town who have either made a profit or need to borrow. Fino, being such a burly giant of a man had immediately appealed to the old money lender as a guard. I think that Fino has found his correct station in life.

§

Diana and Edward decided to cancel the hotel in Florence and to stay at the Monte Ariggio for the rest of the week. Their room was on the second floor and was quite obviously part of the original building. They could both imagine Prince Ned and Isabetta sleeping in the same room looking out onto the Tuscan countryside with its rolling hills and a vineyard laid out mathematically within sight.

When they had showered and changed they went down to dinner expecting a typical Italian menu, but they were both surprised to be offered steak and kidney pie or roast beef and yorkshire pudding. The waiter said that there had always been a tradition that English style food was to be on offer now and then. They chose the house wine again and were pleased with the way it went well with Diana's roast beef and Edward's steak and kidney.

The next morning, Diana wanted to go shopping in Florence and so they took the small Fiat hire-car and parked near the centre before the shops opened. As they were having a coffee together in the Piazza de Domo, Diana asked Edward what he intended to look at next.

'I've run out of ideas for the moment,' he answered, 'just look around you at the crowds and the buildings, it's all such a jungle, where do we start?'

'Don't they have telephone books in Italy? Why don't we just look up the family name and see if there are any around here?' proposed Diana looking archly at her husband as if such an idea was so simple that even an idiot like him could have thought of it.

'You could be on to something there darling. Let's do it.'

They strolled across to the nearest hotel foyer and asked to look at the phone directory. Immediately, Diana found two entries for Scrivano in Florence. They noted down the addresses and found one they could walk to and the other would need the car.

The first was an apartment nearby and they walked up the steps and Edward rang the bell. A woman answered who spoke no English and was obviously mystified by their questions. No man appeared and the whole incident proved embarrassing, so the two left as soon as they could and found the car. The second address was on the road to Fiesole. They found a grander house surrounded by trees and a wall. They stopped at the gate and spoke into a microphone built into the brick gatepost. Edward asked in English if they could speak to signore Scrivano. The gates opened and they drove in. A manservant opened the front door and they were ushered into a pleasant drawing room furnished in a modern style. A well-dressed couple were sitting having coffee and gestured for Edward and Diana to join them.

'Please, what is all this about and how do you know our name?' asked the husband.

Edward then went into his short speech explaining about the journal, but the blank looks on the two faces told the story.

'Has your family always lived in Florence?' asked Diana.

'Yes we think so, but my older brother, Phillipe would know more than me. He is the head of the family now. But he lives in New York,' said the husband, 'I am Marco by the way.'

Edward tried again,

'Do you have any family history stories or a family bible? Anything like that?'

'My brother has all that kind of thing. He may have some stuff from our grandfather, but not here in Italy. He is director of the family company, Orbis.'

Edward leaned forward excitedly,

'Do you mean the company that owns the Monte

Ariggio hotel?'

'Exactly, you have seen it yes?'

'We are staying there.' said Edward.

'I believe that used to be my family home at one time, but we never go there,' said Marco. Edward had a coughing fit at this stage as it was becoming clear that there must be a connection with this couple and the Ned of the journal. But they seemed uninterested to say the least. He supposed that if an Italian couple had arrived on his doorstep in Winchester, with a tale of a book found in another country that might be by a remote ancestor, he might be less than thrilled. This couple were not even historians, he supposed.

'What is your profession sir?' he asked.

'I am a retired business man, I worked for Orbis many years myself as *contabile* an accountant you would say.'

'Well thank-you sir, I am sorry to have troubled you,' said Edward getting up.

'It was nice to meeting you,' said the wife.

As they were leaving the room, Marco spoke again,

'You know, my brother told me of a very old family legend at one time. We believe that many years ago a Scrivano was supposed to have shot a cantalupo with an arrow from an old English bow from the head of his wife for a bet. Like William Tell you know?'

'Thank-you, thank-you so much. That fits the story so well. Can you give me the email address of your brother Phillipe?'

'Absolutely professor,' said Marco and wrote it down on a piece of paper for them.

Edward and Diana thanked the couple profusely and returned to their hire-car very pleased with the encounter.

'That was entirely your idea,' the professor admitted to his wife as they drove back to the Monte Ariggio, 'now we must find out more about the wine.'

Chapter 23

The next day Bishop William arrived home from
London. He was surprised but pleased to see me in his
home. He had been advising the king and the Lords
Appellant on some aspect of church law, but he had also
been making enquiries about Simon Martial and Lisa. It
seems that they had both stopped in Southwark for a day
and the owner of a boarding house reported that they
had a suspiciously heavy chest and four men to help with
them. By the time anyone had taken notice of the
information, they had gone.

I am no longer interested in what happened to Simon. I
am tired and longing to get back home. How strange it is
that my home is now in such a far away place as Italy. It
shows how the world has shrunk since the day I was born.
Soon people born in Arabia may come to live in
England, or English men will make their homes in France
and marry French women? It has happened with royalty,
why not with yeomen? Fino and I will ride to
Southampton tomorrow and board *Vivandi*. I know that
Giuseppe will be pleased to get home too. He has a wife
and three children in Genoa.

***

What a pleasure it is to be with family and friends again. Ralf has bought two fine new horses including a stallion that will increase the value of our stock. Matthias has proved his loyalty and worth by helping to bottle more wine and to take several barrels to market in Firenze. Both my little boys are healthy and bouncing all over the place, but best of all, my Isabetta welcomes me with loving kisses and embraces which draw us even closer together.

I have been thinking internationally recently, and I would like to export more silks and wine to other parts of the *mare nostrum*. I also intend to import more wool. I shall call my new enterprise "Mondo" meaning we span the whole world. Captain Giuseppe Esposito agrees with me and I am inclined to purchase two or more vessels and appoint him as Commodore of my fleet. There are opportunities in the north of Africa and the Holy Land I am sure. The Medici brothers are keen to support this idea. It may be possible to start another bank abroad if I can find trustworthy people to run it.

It is now the year of our Lord 1390. I have brought back from England a copy of Geoffrey Chaucer's Canterbury Tales, published only three or four years agon and as yet unknown in Italy. It is an entertaining book, the like of which has never been seen. We are so fortunate to be living in such modern times as these. I look forward to taking my sons to sea with me to experience travel and other countries' manners. It will be this sort of education that will keep my family business expanding and feeding us all.

§

Signora Voltolini was unable to help with any information about the wine. She said they had always served it in the hotel and that although there was a small vineyard attached to the property, the wine was made from grapes grown in the Orbis vineyards all over Italy. It was mainly bottled in a company establishment in Florence, that's all she knew.

It was time for the Clarks to go home.

Edward was very satisfied with his discoveries and was determined to contact the brother Phillipe Scrivana when he got back to his office. The whole thing was a marvellous tale of achievement over the centuries. It was amazing that through a 13th century document the origins of a global company could be traced. How many other enterprises were there in the world that might perhaps be attributable in the same way but for which no evidence existed?

They returned the hire car and took the train back to Rome. They arrived in Winchester in the pouring rain yet were both pleased to be back under a dark English sky. Edward had brought two bottles of the Monte Ariggio wine in his hand luggage, one to give to the Vice Chancellor Julian Smart, as a sort of proof of the connection of Italy with Winchester. He was exhausted from the trip and less inclined to want to write about it than he had been originally. Diana had two new dresses from the Rome visit and a packet of Italian coffee from Florence.

Edward rang the the Rev Brian Woodward to tell him briefly about his discoveries and the justification of Ned Scrivener's existence and the global company that he seems to have started. The Dean was elated to hear the news, as it seemed to him that the monetary value of the journal must go up as a result.

There was a message on his office answer phone from Amelia Gillies to welcome him back and to say that she was engaged to Tristan Smallwood and it was not appropriate for them to see one another any more. It was no more than Edward had been expecting so he mentally shrugged and got on with the work that had piled up in his absence.

§

It is now five years since my last entry in this journal. This year is 1395 and I believe I am thirty summers old. Life has been so busy that I seem to have had no time to write my thoughts. My son Justin is ten years old and my Piero is seven and Roberto five. Matthias came to me last year and offered to tutor both boys to read and write in

Italian and Latin. I have been teaching them English myself. I have also fashioned small longbows and arrows for them and they are becoming quite proficient. I have told them the tale of their mother and the melon on her head many times, because they can never hear enough of my stories.

At last, I am of the view that it is too fanciful to continue with a diary such as this. I am too busy and also not of noble birth and of no account in the eyes of God. It has been perhaps too presumptuous of me to write it. I shall send it to Winchester to my old friend Athelstan who made this book for me, and ask him to hide it somewhere suitable. He cannot read and he will lock it safely. Someone may perhaps discover it in 50 years time and find it of interest. I will ask Piero and Roberto to sign on this final page to show that they are the next generation of this family here in Tuscany.

Roberto Scrivener

Piero Scrivener

Ned Scrivener

§

The Dean had made all the preparations he could think of for the sale of the journal. He had paid for a glossy brochure to be printed and mailed it across the world to all the people he thought might be responsive. He had received emails and letters from a dozen or more collectors and academics who were intrigued. He had asked Edward to write a page about his discoveries in Italy to add an extra spice to the story. Now all he could do was to wait and see. Whatever happened, he thought, surely the Cathedral will benefit.

The day arrived and Sothebys were finally holding an auction of ancient books and manuscripts in London. The journal had created a lot of interest and was illustrated on the cover of the Sothebys' catalogue. The Dean, Smallwood and Amelia, as well as Edward and Diana Clarke had travelled up to London to make an occasion of it and to attend the auction.

As always there was an electric atmosphere in the sale room from the start. There were about 150 items to be sold ranging from a letter from Winston Churchill to a Chinese scroll of such antiquity that it had to be kept in a glass case. When Ned Scrivener's journal came up it was held high in an assistant's hand, unprotected and looking good. The auctioneer began by asking half a million pounds, the next bid was one million without a pause. Two people in the room began vying with one another, two and a half, three million, a pause while a telephone bid was taken for three and a half million pounds. Four million came from the floor. There was another pause and the telephone bid shot up to five million pounds, and the auctioneer asked for more, but heads shook and the telephone bid took it for five million.

The Dean was ecstatic and stood up from his seat clapping.

'Who was the bidder?' whispered Edward.

'No idea,' said the Dean, 'I don't mind who it is. The cathedral is better off by five million pounds.'

Edward approached the auctioneer when the sale was over and asked about the bidder for the journal.

'It was a corporate bid from New York, a Prince Ariggio de Monte,' he said, 'no-one I've ever heard of.'

The End

18677206R00106

Printed in Poland
by Amazon Fulfillment
Poland Sp. z o.o., Wrocław